YOU ARE POWERFUL

THE SECRET

YOU ARE

TO EVERYDAY

POWERFUL

MANIFESTATION

BECKI RABIN

POP PRESS

Published in 2021 by Pop Press, an imprint of Ebury Publishing,
20 Vauxhall Bridge Road,
London SW1V 2SA

Pop Press is part of the Penguin Random House group of companies
whose addresses can be found at global.penguinrandomhouse.com

Penguin
Random House
UK

First published by Pop Press in 2021

www.penguin.co.uk

A CIP catalogue record for this book is available from the British Library

ISBN 9781529148275

Design by Imagist

Typeset in 9/12 pt Neuzeit Office Pro by Jouve (UK), Milton Keynes
Printed and bound in Great Britain by Clays Ltd, Elcograf S.p.A.

The authorised representative in the EEA is Penguin Random
House Ireland, Morrison Chambers, 32 Nassau Street, Dublin
D02 YH68.

Contents

Introducing the Power of Manifestation

You are powerful, my love . . .

Would you believe me if I told you that there is a version of you that's a little shinier round the edges? One that is confident, happy, fulfilled and believes they are capable of absolutely anything – wait, let me rephrase that – *deserving* of everything? How about if I told you that there is a life available to you full of all the fabulous things you want?

You may not believe yet that you can create your dream reality, but the truth is you are incredibly powerful. More than you know. And the best part? That power isn't something you must go looking for or spend a lifetime trying to win. It isn't something outside of you and it certainly isn't only available to a special few. Your power is already there, buried within you. All you've got to do is dust off the cobwebs and switch the light back on so that you can radiate your innate inner power, shine bright and call in what you want in life. You are the artist of the picture of your life. You paint everything that you experience, feel, have and own in your world.

MAKING IT HAPPEN

If I'm completely honest with you, this whole self-help thing was never my bag. It all seemed a bit much, the idea that we are immensely powerful and there is something out there bigger than all of us. When it came to manifesting, I found the whole thing a little far-fetched and confusing. The idea that I had power to attract what I wanted seemed like something you only read about in books. Sure, the concept was great in theory, but how the hell did you make it happen? Do you just close your eyes and see it and – boom – it appears? Do you say a sentence and that's it – you step through the cupboard into a Narnia where you're richer, prettier, happier and more successful?

Maybe you are like I was and unsure if you buy into the idea of manifesting, or maybe there is this voice telling you it isn't available to you; that it is only for the special ones with 'woo-woo' superpowers, the spiritual sistas on yoga retreats. The same voice that, now you come to think of it, tells you a lot of things aren't available to you and always finds a way to get you to sit back down every time you even so much as *think* about getting up to shine.

You are not alone, girl – I have her inside of me too. I call her Self-sabotaging Susan but you may call her whatever you like. For years, she ruled my life, kept me small, kept me 'safe', kept me going back to situations that left me feeling low, shameful, guilty and undeserving. Convincing me that a greater, more fulfilling life wasn't available to me. That manifesting wasn't available to me.

Well, let me tell you something: manifesting your dream life is absolutely available to you! I believe we all have a power that – when we connect to it, own it and embrace it – makes us attractive AF. People want to be around us; good things are drawn to us and we become magnets for the good that life has to offer. When we accept our power and own it, we feel lovely, confident, capable and deserving of a good life. Things always seem to go our way and we get what we want. On the other hand, when we aren't connected to our power, we feel stressed, anxious, fearful and unsupported. Our energy is low, our lights are off – it feels like nobody is home and the world is against us.

I am here to help you unlearn all the lessons that taught you that you aren't powerful, capable, deserving and special, and to help you connect to that power of yours and speed up your manifestations. You see, everything I have now in my life, I manifested. Even before I realised I was doing it, I was. Big things like where and how I live and my work, but also the little things, like how my day unfolds and the people I meet. I manifested it all. When I got over all of the excuses, distractions and confusion, and learnt just how powerful manifestation can be, I decided to live my life in a way that meant I manifested epic things.

If you want to manifest in the most spectacular way possible, attracting only good things into your life, then first you must rise up from the depths of self-doubt, fear, worry and anger. You must break free from old, conditioned thinking and those patterns and beliefs that keep you focused on what you *don't* have in your life. You have to take responsibility for your energy rising all the way up to your highest, brightest setting – this is where you feel content, happy, confident and grateful for all that you have in your life already.

Learning to manifest isn't some sacred secret. It is learning to live life in a certain way, to embody a certain version of yourself – a version that I am going to help you step into through the pages of this book. The advice I will be sharing with you changed my life. When I implemented this way of living, I created a life that feels freaking good. Yes, I face challenges. Yes, I still question myself. But I know how to choose another way and thrive. I learnt to use my power in ways that made me feel good and brought good things into my life – things I'd been dreaming about since I was a child, like writing this book.

The principles in this book are those I have learnt over the years as a coach, working with thousands of women while on my own journey of self-discovery. They helped take me from the depths of depression to a place I never thought I would reach. When I dusted off the cobwebs and found my power within, everything changed. I went from being knee-deep in self-hate, uncertainty and anxiety to a life that is full of joy, excitement and clarity. From feeling like life was working against me to literally jumping out of bed each day. While I don't have everything sussed (who does?), I want you to know that if I can do it, so can you.

In the first part of this book, I will give you my framework for understanding how manifesting works, what it truly is and what's essential to know when starting out on your manifesting journey. Then, in the second part, I am going to give you ten manifesting principles with simple exercises to help you put each one into practice. These are the secrets I wish I'd been given as a young girl. Some of these exercises might ask you to implement new rituals or embody new ways of living; for those that ask you questions, you might want to jot down your answers in a sparkly new journal or you can do it in the note pages at the back of this book.

Whatever the reason that brought you here – whether a niggle told you to take peek at these pages, or a friend insisted you take a look, or you simply need a little reminder of just how powerful you are – trust that you are here for a purpose and you are meant to be reading this book right now. I hope from the bottom of my heart that the principles that follow will help give you clarity and the strength to rise up to your highest self and fullest potential so that you become super-attractive to all that you dream of in life.

You can read this book once front to back or you can pull it out whenever you need a little reminder of just how freaking powerful you are. I will always be here hyping you up and cheering you on from the sidelines. You, my love, are powerful beyond measure. Please read these pages over and over until you believe it. The world needs your light.

What is Manifesting?

When you feel good, good things happen.

When people talk about the practice of 'manifesting' today, they mean creating our own reality by being a magnet for all that we want to feel, have and experience in our lives. To give it to you short and sweet, your ability to manifest comes from the energy you create with your thoughts, actions and beliefs. For me, manifesting all the lovely things you want from your life means becoming the most lit-up version of yourself. When you rise up, right up, to your fullest potential and get good at feeling good, you begin to vibrate at a higher frequency, giving off a positive energy – and so, with the help of a few rituals, manifesting positive things becomes the natural outcome.

Manifesting is often misunderstood. Typically, I find that confusion often exists in two areas:

1. People think it is only available to a select few.
2. People think it means *only* getting what you *want*.

The truth is that manifesting isn't only available to a special few; everyone is manifesting their reality. There is no spiritual gift or qualification you need to be able to manifest. You already have everything you need.

While, yes, we can use the principles of manifesting to create our desired reality – and my plan is absolutely to help you do that – what most people don't realise is that you are actually always manifesting, every single day in every single moment, so it's important to understand that you can manifest negative things too. The reality you are living right now as you read this book – you made it happen. You created it with your thoughts, your beliefs, your actions and your vibrational frequency (energy). Yep, the life you lead right now, you manifested it. Wherever you are as you read this, whatever your life looks like – you did that. That is why I sometimes like to call this practice 'creating' instead of manifesting.

How you think directly links to what you attract.

Your outside world as you know it now is a reflection of your inner world – what you think, feel, say and what you habitually do. Your thinking, beliefs and feelings are the guiding framework to the reality you are creating and living in any moment. It is all linked to how you think about yourself, the world and what is available to you. Your thoughts are one of the most powerful manifesting tools you have. Why? Because they have a snowball effect on everything.

Here's how it works. When we have a thought repeatedly (which we often do), it gets stronger until it eventually become a belief. Beliefs tend to be deep rooted and stick around longer than thoughts. Both thoughts and beliefs are charged with emotions such as happiness or sadness, which in turn cause us to make certain choices and behave in certain ways. The actions we then take affect what happens in our reality. This is the basic principle of manifestation:

Thoughts affect your feelings, which affect your behaviour = your reality

Let me give you an example. Let's be honest, most women at some point have had the thought 'I am not pretty enough'. If you haven't, I salute you! But if you have the thought repeatedly that you aren't pretty, it is likely to become a firm belief. And how will that make you feel? Pretty shitty, right? Shameful and sad.

So, how are you going to act if you think you aren't pretty? You are likely to hide and play small. You won't post that picture in case somebody says something nasty; you won't approach people you're interested in because you think they will reject you. You won't get up on stage in front of groups to fulfil your dream in case people notice how 'ugly' you are. And guess what? Your reality doesn't change. *You take no action, so you get no results.* Your initial thought created your reality and results in an eternal vicious cycle.

Our thoughts and beliefs are formed from our memories and experiences of pivotal moments in our life as well as the things we heard, saw and learnt from the people around us. These learnings form our subconscious programming and become imprinted within our conditioned mind over time, and impact our everyday behaviour.

MY STORY

Let's look at the formation of some of my subconscious beliefs and how they then affected my reality to give you an example of what I mean . . . I was born into this world with quite the story. The same day my parents found out that they were expecting me, they also found out that my dad's heart was deteriorating and he wasn't eligible for a transplant. On 27 August 1989, my father passed away, just ten days before I made it into this world. I missed that cuddle by the skin of my teeth. A cuddle that I now know might have changed my entire belief system.

While I know that I brought joy into my family's life, giving them hope and light, grief was inevitably all around us. From the earliest stages of my life, I saw the constant battle my sister and mum faced every day, cherishing a newborn while grieving a father and husband. My mum went into survival mode and worked 24/7 to earn enough to support us as a family. As I grew older, I saw her work and work to survive; I saw her struggle to overcome the pain of loss while enjoying the love of new life. I saw her suffer as, to her, life felt unfair.

At the same, without realising it, I felt that my dad didn't think it was worth sticking around for a few more days to meet me, so I felt rejected. The ages 0–7 are when most of our conditioning takes place. At those ages, I subconsciously learnt the following:

- From being born into this world in a place of grief, my mind learnt that *with the birth of a baby comes death elsewhere.*
- By having a father who left me before he met me, I learnt that *men always leave and that I wasn't enough to hold on too.*
- In watching my mum work all hours to make money for us to survive, I learnt that *the only way to earn money was to hustle and overwork to the point of breakdown.*
- In hearing my mum talk of the pain, stress and struggle she had to endure to support us, I learnt that *success and wealth come with pain and struggle and stress always has to be our driving force.*

These experiences shaped how I believed life should look and what was available to me, which in turn became the blueprint for my money story, my relationship story and my career story. It became ingrained in my subconscious mind and thus the framework for the life I led and what I manifested into my reality.

As a result, I attracted guys I knew would leave or pushed them away so they had to leave – I believed they were going to do it anyway and being left was a role I knew how to play. I overworked and yet never earnt to my full potential because I thought with wealth came stress and hatred from others. Those are just some of the beliefs that shaped how my reality looked.

You too may find certain things easier or harder to manifest than others. It all depends on the experiences, beliefs and traumas attached to what you want to attract. Some beliefs are especially hard to break free from because a great deal of hurt is linked to them. While those who have experienced less suffering associated with a particular area of their life will often find there is less 'work' to do to change their beliefs, and they can therefore call in what they want in that area more quickly. Take relationships, for example: someone who has endured a lot of heartache may find their relationship manifestations take longer than someone who has experienced relatively little emotional pain.

YOUR STORY

We all have experiences and hardships that become part of our story and our identity. You do, too. They form the blueprint of our conditioning, which dictates the way we think, how we feel, show up and what we believe we deserve. Beginning to understand how my own story shaped my thinking and, thus, my reality, was the start of my manifesting journey. Awareness is one of the first steps in making change and it is incredibly important to become aware of how your experiences have shaped your thinking and your reality.

WHAT IS YOUR STORY?

Have a think about how your own story has shaped your reality and your behaviours:

- · How do you perceive money, work, relationships and what is available to you?
- · Where could these beliefs have originated?
- · What beliefs do you hold about yourself as a person?
- · How have these beliefs affected the way you act and thus your reality?

If you feel you need any further support around these questions or previous experiences, please head to the resources section at the end of the book for some guidance on how the team at GETLIT can help you.

Raising your vibe is the key to manifesting.

If you want to manifest, it is time to surrender to the idea that there is something far bigger at play here than all of us. For years, I tried to ignore the idea that there is an energetic force, a 'higher power' that makes things happen. A force that can't be seen or heard, or even described, but which nonetheless exists. It's what makes the tides flow, the sun shine and the flowers grow – and the same power makes you bump into that person you were just thinking about or see a quote on your social feed at the exact moment you needed it. In some religions, they call it God; in spiritual groups, they may call it Source; in science, they call it energy. Throughout this book, I will be using the word 'Universe' to refer to the powerful energetic force around us, which supports creation.

Our world as we know it and all the living things within it are made of energy and emit a vibrational frequency. Everything vibrates: the world and the things within it. And you, my love, are a powerful thing. You are part of this energetic force, just like everything else; you have your own vibrational frequency, a vibe that you beam into the world, your vibe is a vital tool that will allow you to access your manifesting potential. I cannot express how important it is that you take responsibility for your energy and fiercely protect it. It is freaking powerful stuff. Your vibe speaks to the world and the world meets you there.

WHAT MAKES UP YOUR ENERGY?

You know those super-powerful thoughts, beliefs and feelings that we spoke about earlier? Well, they just got even more powerful because they dictate the vibe you send out into the world. Every single thought and feeling holds a vibrational frequency and the following rule applies: positive, happy and joyful thoughts emit a higher, faster vibration, while the lower, negative and limiting ones have slow, small vibrations.

In his book *Power Vs Force*, Dr David R. Hawkins introduces the 'Level of Consciousness Scale' to identify how our emotional state can impact the way our life unfolds. Inside the cover of this book, you will find my interpretation of this scale. Dr Hawkins highlights how emotions such as fear, worry, shame, guilt and anger are low-vibe (slower frequency) feelings, which leave us stuck, closed off, resistant and repellent to high-vibe things. As we rise up the scale, we move through emotions such as courage, acceptance, neutrality and reason to reach those at the top: love, joy, peace and enlightenment.

When we choose higher-vibe emotions, we raise our vibration and our potential expands. We go from trying to force things, worrying and being fearful, to being more open and flowing – and thus connected to our power. We cease taking incorrect action or little action and begin a productive way of living that makes space for wonderful things to occur. We go from being 'unconscious', where it feels like we are sleepwalking, on autopilot and disconnected from ourselves, at the mercy of our critical mind and limitations, to becoming 'conscious', aware and present.

YOUR VIBE SPEAKS TO THE WORLD

The day I found out about how important my vibe is to what my reality looks like and what I manifest was the day my life changed. It was Christmas 2018 and I was on a month-long trip around Australia with my mum. But instead of taking in the incredible, once-in-a-lifetime scenery of the Great Barrier Reef, I was stressing about whether they would have gluten-free, paleo food onboard the seaplane. Instead of taking a moment to wonder at the insane beauty of the Whitsundays' beaches, I was snapping 1,001 photos to try to get 'that one good picture' – and failing miserably because I wanted to break down and cry at how much I hated how I looked in each one.

I was in the midst of what I call one of my most *Unlit* times in life. As low a vibe as it gets. I was two years post a gut-wrenching break-up that rocked my world and pushed me into a dark hole of depression and it felt like the world hated me, drama was attracted to me and everything was going wrong. I was full of self-hate, talking to myself and treating myself horribly while letting my fear of being too much, or not enough for everyone, win.

Roughly halfway through the trip, I found myself reading one of the most profound books I have ever read, which was to shape my whole future. I was about three years into my personal development work and had started to dig deep into all that was holding me back, but still nothing was really shifting. However, *There's a Spiritual Solution to Every Problem* by the late Dr Wayne W. Dyer hit me differently. It fell into my lap at the perfect moment. I was finally ready to let the words sink in.

In the book, Dr Dyer talks about how energy affects reality.

Dr Dyer says that faster vibrations attract higher vibe things (possibilities), while lower vibrations attract lower vibe things (problems). And that you, and only you, are responsible for the energy of your life because you are made of energy too.

Our individual frequencies travel at different speeds depending on what we are doing and how we feel, and that frequency acts as a kind of magnet. We all know a person who regularly says 'trust that bad thing to happen to me'. They are always the one who bad things actually happen to, right? It is all in their energy. They aren't beaming with good vibes, so shadow shit is being thrown their way. We have probably all met someone and thought, 'I just don't like her, though I don't know why.' Whether we notice it or not, we are drawn to or repelled by other people's energy.

Essentially, when it comes to manifesting, the higher your vibe, the more attractive you are to the higher vibe stuff (like the very things and people you desire). The lower your vibe, the more problems you face. Good things are drawn to those who radiate and beam the brightest, and we are naturally drawn to them, too. People want to sunbathe in that light. It's pretty simple – but life changing.

COMMIT TO A HIGH-VIBE LIFE

That time in Australia, I was operating from the lowest of my vibes, living in these low feelings: *shame* for feeling like a fraud, *fear* of being who I really wanted to be, *guilt* around my food and exercise and *anger* at all the pain I had been through with relationships. It was an endless cycle of low-vibe stuff. And I was attracting things that matched that vibration.

It's rare that I work with a woman who hasn't spent much of her life operating from those low-vibe feelings. From there, my love, it is impossible to create a good life. It is impossible to positively create. We cannot live in low-vibe emotions and still attract high-vibe things. It doesn't work like that. You attract the vibrational match for the vibe you are emitting.

When we commit to the high vibe, we get a good life. We become attractive: people chase us; things chase us. Imagine breaking up with someone and spending a few weeks crying, being all needy and sad (low vibe). Your ex runs a mile, likely repelled by your low energy. Then one day you wake up and realise you are a badass, your ex is a loser and you deserve SO much more – you begin to glow and all of a sudden your ex comes crawling back, tail between legs. We've all been there. This couldn't show more clearly how powerful energy is: *we smell good when we feel good.*

Throughout our lives, we move up and down the scale and the energy we emit will change, impacting what we are able to attract and manifest. We can't be at the top of our game all the time, right? It wouldn't make sense or be humanly feasible. But what we can do is dedicate as much time as we can to those thoughts and behaviours that keep us as high up that scale as possible. Then, when we do find ourselves in a low-vibe situation or face a problem, we are armed with the tools to get back up and shine.

WHAT ARE YOU MANIFESTING RIGHT NOW?

To help you identify where your own vibration currently sits on the scale, I have identified the four fundamental levels of 'being' that impact our manifesting potential. Read the following descriptions and take note of your most common emotions, thoughts, beliefs and habits, which will reveal the current manifesting level of your energy.

LEVEL 4: LIVING IN SUFFERING AND SHAME

At this level, you often feel like life is against you and good things don't happen to you like they do for others. You are living in what seems like a world of challenges and problems, and it feels like you never get a break from things going wrong. You hold a lot of shame and often indulge in critical chatter. Critical of yourself, the world around you, others and what is available to you. Self-love feels far away and perhaps you are hurting from a painful experience, regret your actions or have suffered loss. Life may feel heavy, as though you cannot see the light. At this level, we often cling to past hurts, upset or disappointments.

Key emotions: shame, guilt, fear and grief.

Manifesting potential: at this level, we are what I call 'living in lack', with a victim mentality. Much of our thinking is focused on the 'withouts' and what is 'wrong' or could go wrong in our life. When it comes to manifesting, our vibe is so low that we manifest problems, not good stuff. We are a vibrational match for low-vibe things.

LEVEL 3: LIVING FOR APPROVAL

At this level, you may be driven by your achievements, appearance and accolades. Being important, successful and noticed are essential for you and your happiness. Validation is key – you feel seen and appreciated when others give you a pat on the back. You may question how you are perceived by others and wanting things to be perfect is important to you, which can lead to comparison with others and resentment or jealousy over what they have and you don't. Anxious thoughts, worries and fears often keep you stuck and afraid of making changes, even when you want to. You fear others may judge you and you focus on what could go wrong if you don't achieve what you are working hard to make happen.

Key emotions: desire, fear, anger.

Manifesting potential: you may wonder why you aren't attracting all you want. On the outside, it seems like you are connecting with your higher self because you are 'achieving'; however, when you look a little deeper, you are relying on other people, things or accolades to make yourself feel complete and worthy. I call this state the 'approval seeker'. I sat in this frequency for a long time, wondering why I wasn't manifesting, but I was giving away my power to everything else. I thought feeling good came when I hit a milestone or was told by somebody that I was good. The problem with this state is that you are living in fear. Fear that you won't be enough for people or liked unless you are a certain way. Fear that you won't succeed. We lose our authenticity and, more importantly, we give away our manifesting powers to others.

LEVEL 2: LIVING WITH ACCEPTANCE AND NEUTRALITY

At this stage, you have started to accept yourself for who you are. You feel neutral towards a lot of things, content with the smaller stuff in life and mostly at peace. Though you aren't free from worries or problems and you find yourself slipping back into level four or three regularly. However, life is good and you always find a way to come back to your contentment. You have learnt the art of forgiveness and are beginning to trust in the lessons of your past experiences, hopeful that the future looks bright for you. You are pretty accepting of the life you have, although you know there is more out there for you and you are grateful for all that is.

Key emotions: acceptance, willingness, neutrality and courage.

Manifesting potential: you are on your way to manifesting good things. You have started to understand that the power lies within you; you take responsibility for your actions and beliefs and know that you have the ability to create a good life. When you are hopeful, forgiving, trusting and content, you become a vibrational match for good things.

LEVEL 1: THE LIT-UP LIFE

At this highest level, you feel that when problems arise you can let them pass; you don't judge yourself for having them and you let yourself experience your emotions before quickly falling back into a loving mindset. You find the lessons in most situations and you are always on the hunt for the positives and possibilities in life. You get a deep sense of fulfilment and joy from serving others, which comes from a place of passion rather than a need for validation. You are not particularly concerned about what people think of you and outcomes. Instead, you focus on living in the moment, grateful for all that you have. Your primary drive is less about approval and more about peace. You implement practices that help you connect to your power and have a deep sense of self-awareness. Your life feels like it has a purpose and you protect your energy by giving it to things that make you feel good. You know that you are whole and complete just as you are. You love, respect and care for yourself; you know you are best for others when you have prioritised being the best for you.

Key emotions: peace, love, joy, fulfilment and even moments of enlightenment.

Manifesting potential: you got it! This is where you are connected to your power and ready to make your wishes come true. Your vibration is high vibe and you attract high-vibe things. These come to you without much effort and you are very good at getting what you want.

Level 1 is where we want to be mainly operating from. This is when we embody our higher self and are well on the way to being in a place where we can receive all that we want in life. For a long time, I was stuck around level four, dipping my toe into level three occasionally and two if I was feeling wild. Now, I operate mainly in levels one and two. From time to time, I wobble when my old triggers hit me in certain areas of life and I can find myself operating out of level four and three again. *That is totally normal* – you too may flip between the different levels and that's totally OK.

That's the great thing about your energy – when you become aware of it, you can shift it at any moment and make a commitment to change. I am going to show you how to do that throughout this book, but on the next page is a mantra (a positive statement) to help you get started by raising your vibe.

BE A MAGNET FOR GOOD

Close your eyes, take a deep breath, place your hands on your heart and connect to your breath for a minute. Internally smile to yourself and repeat the words below three times:

'I am ready to commit to raising my vibration and rising. I am now embodying the true light that I am and am connected to my power. I am a magnet for all that is good because I have changed my energy.'

Keep repeating this five times a day for as long as you like. It feels good to feel good, right? Feeling good is the secret formula to attracting good.

The principles laid out in the next part of this book are some of my everyday secrets that will help you take responsibility for raising and protecting your energy, support you on your mission to feel truly good and give you the guidance to help you rise up so that you too can create a good life.

You Are Capable of Powerful Things

A shinier version of you exists. Find her and embrace your power.

People who are good at manifesting all have one thing in common: a belief in the 'self'. Self-worth, self-acceptance, self-respect, self-love – they all start with the same word. These people have an innate knowledge that they are enough just as they are and that they are worthy of all they desire. You cannot outsmart your self-worth – it is the root of everything. If you truly want to attract all of those shiny new relationships, careers, homes, friendships and finances, you have to believe you are worthy of whatever it is that you want – and you have to believe that you can create it.

The very first principle is pretty simple but essential. I need you to get comfortable with the idea of rising up to your highest, most expanded self. Get comfortable with believing that version of you even exists. Get comfortable with knowing how powerful you are. Even when the world tells you that you aren't.

There are three essential elements to getting comfortable with the idea of raising your vibe and connecting to your power, so let's look at them next.

BELIEVE IN YOUR HIGHER SELF

The first thing I need you to do is get up, stand front of the mirror, look yourself in the eye and say to yourself: 'I believe in my higher self.' You must believe in a version of yourself that is free from self-doubt, worry, fear and shame; a version of you who can have and be whoever and whatever you want. If you don't believe in her, she won't shine. None of the practices in this book will work if you don't believe it's possible. All I am asking of you, right now, is to believe she exists; the rest I will help you with.

For many of us, self-love feels impossible. It did for me too until I started working on my self-acceptance and, as I began to become more accepting of myself, it became easier to rise my vibes day by day. Over time, it became natural. As you follow some of the following principles, you will work out your self-worth muscle. Instinctively and subconsciously, your self-worth will rise and so will your ability to attract wonderful things. When you believe it, you can start your journey to becoming it.

SAY IT LIKE YOU MEAN IT

Write down the following affirmations and repeat them out loud three or four times a day until they sink in:

'I am brilliant, deserving, capable and worthy of having a good life.'

'I am deserving of feeling good, committed to feeling good and feel comfortable feeling good.'

'I am excited to become the best version of myself.'

'I choose to see life through the lens of love, happiness, joy, possibilities and peace.'

IT IS YOUR BIRTHRIGHT TO SHINE

Let me tell you something: you are not serving anyone by shrinking yourself down and playing small, hiding in the shadows. It is not self-indulgent, diva-ish or stuck up to love yourself and shine your light. In fact, shining is your birthright and we need more women to know that is OK to turn on their light.

Somewhere along the way, many of us have got caught up in the lie that we have to wait for others to give us permission to shine. That it is wrong to turn our lights all the way up and show up for the world as our brightest self. I see it with every single one of the wonderful women I work with. Their worries aren't that they aren't capable or talented enough to get that job or start their business. Most know deep down how talented they are but worry what people might say or if they might fail. Their fear is not of their capability but of being seen – of shining bright. It was a revelation for me when I realised that was my deepest fear, too.

My childhood dream was to be in a girl band. I spent hours prancing around my bedroom, singing along to Destiny's Child and pretending I was in a huge arena performing to thousands. That was my happy place. I will never forget the day I was singing at school when my teacher shouted out, 'Stop showing off, Rebecca – nobody likes a show-off.' At the tender age of ten, I was told that it wasn't OK to shine, that it wasn't OK to be the centre of attention. I learnt there and then that I would be hated for showing my talents and doing what I love.

Let's face it, our society is set up to teach us that loving ourselves or 'showing off' is self-indulgent and vain. The sense of unlimited capacity we have as children gets crushed by the lies we are sold about our worthiness to shine. As a result, nobody wants to be the girl who loves herself too much. Nobody wants to stand out a little bit more than anyone else because then we are noticed and can be ridiculed, rejected.

My secondary school's motto was 'Let your light shine'; it was printed on my school jumper and sung at every assembly. Yet I spent the vast majority of my life fanny-assing around with the switch. I never truly stepped into my power. I always hid behind others, worrying whether people would think I was arrogant, if they would laugh at me – would I get it wrong, was I even any good? In my early stages of entrepreneurship, I hid behind my business partners, my clients, my peers. I filled myself up with so many limiting beliefs that I prevented myself from even trying. I let my fear of being seen, my fear of failure, my fear of my own goddamn magic and my belief it wasn't OK to shine hold me back from achieving all the things I wanted for far too long. I mistook this for so many other things – like lack of confidence, anxiety, low self-esteem – but it really was just my fear of allowing my talents to shine.

We will take a look at your fears later and how to reframe them, but right now, I need us to make a pledge together. I need you to know that it is OK to shine. It is literally your birthright to shine. Your light is your most natural state. It is the immense power in you, it is your extraordinary potential, your calling, your purpose. None of us were born with brighter lights than another, with greater purposes or more successful paths laid out – that isn't how this works. We all have the same capacity to shine.

So if you are waiting for someone to give you permission – here it is. It is OK to light yourself all the way up, my love. So. Freaking. OK.

YOU ARE COMPLETE AS YOU ARE

I am going to let you into one of the biggest mistakes people make when it comes to trying to manifest. When people start to get interested in the idea of manifesting, it's mostly because they want change. Right? Something has prompted you to change the way your current reality looks. The problem with this is that sometimes your motivation can be coming from a place of feeling incomplete, and that is a low-vibe feeling.

People often think that a change will fix things, make them feel whole and complete their happiness. That only when we get X will we be happy – when we call in that relationship, then we will feel loved; when we get that dream career, then we will become successful; when we have the perfect body, then we will be adored. But this means we are giving our power away. We give the power to all of those *things* to complete us. To make us whole. As though there is a part of us that is incomplete. Can you see the even bigger problem here? It's that if those things disappear, or we don't achieve them, then our self-worth, love, happiness and all the other emotions we've attached to them walk out of the door too.

It's time to take back that power: you are whole and complete as you are, in this moment. You can feel all those things you hope to gain from your manifestations whenever you want to, including right now. When you realise this, what you desire from life changes. The reasons behind your manifestations change. You seek only things that will add to your life, instead trying to fill the voids. The voids don't really exist: you already are loved, you already are whole, you already are complete. No relationship, job, or material item will do that for you. When we know that we are whole, regardless of whatever else happens or what we have in our life, our energy shifts into a more peaceful, high-vibe and trusting energy. And remember where peace is on the scale? Right there at the top. Attractive AF.

As you work through this book and start to get clear about what it is that you want, ask yourself why you want it, what is the energy behind it. Is it to make yourself feel complete? Fill a void? To make you feel loved? Is there a sense of lack behind it? Remember, we cannot manifest from a place of lack. So if you are looking for someone to make you feel loved, love yourself. If you are looking for something to make you safe and secure, create your own safety. Take back the power.

Stand up to Self-sabotaging Susan

Choose feeling happy over feeling crappy.

There is a part of you that isn't really you. Not the real you, anyway. It is a part of yourself that holds onto your old beliefs and traumas in an attempt to keep you safe from rejection or potential failure. You may have heard people talk of the ego and living in our egoic mind. Psychologists call it our critical mind; coaches call it our inner critic or our shadow side. It is usually all referring the same thing. As I mentioned her earlier, I call her Susan. I have friends who call theirs Dave; you may call yours whatever you wish. When I listen to Susan's voice above my own, I know that I am resisting my creating power.

How do we know when our inner critic is in charge? It's simple. The inner critic is that loud voice that sounds like it is shouting you. She constantly wants you to prove your importance and pushes you to show you're superior to others. She is also often the one telling you that you can't or shouldn't do something. She's responsible for many of our self-defeating thoughts about how unworthy we are, how silly for even thinking great things are possible. She is usually the one who makes us overthink things or obsess over all that we do not have or cannot do. She thrives in moments of self-doubt, neglect or sorrow. She is the one that keeps us in our shadows.

She sounds like a total bitch, I know, but she doesn't do this because she doesn't like you or want you to succeed. She does it because her role is to keep you safe. She likes the familiar and rejects anything that is unknown or puts you in a situation where you are subject to anything risky. So, really, her intentions are pure. The issue is, in doing all of this, she keeps you at a low vibe and causes you to neglect and limit your most powerful self.

Your higher self, however, has a much quieter voice and while she shines bright when she is in the spotlight, she does not require or desire the light. She speaks in soft, one-word answers, with a simple yes or no. She is the gut feeling that often can't be explained and gives you a feeling of pure knowing. She is your shine.

When offering women business mentoring, I have come across a recurring theme: just before they were about to launch a new project or product, they would sabotage themselves. They would somehow allow a problem to get in the way. They would fall ill, relapse into old patterns like negative self-talk or panic attacks or get stuck in a painful situation somewhere in their life. All in the bid to stay safe, to stop themselves shining. And guess what? When this sabotage worked, they had all the proof they needed – evidence that supported their original limiting belief that they weren't worthy of launching a business. And the cycle goes back round and around.

So how do we beat this voice? Well, here's the thing. Trying to beat your inner critic, your Susan, is actually exactly what she would tell you to do: that is the ego's answer to solving the problem – *beat her*. But beating her isn't essential; there is no need to hate her. After all, she is where your biggest fears lie. Instead, we need to nurture her, reprogramme her, become aware of when she is at play and let her know that it is safe to choose the shinier version of you instead. You then need to nurture your higher self so that she can confidently take her rightful place in the light.

Here are four ways to start standing up to your inner critic and nurture the higher version of yourself, who knows just how powerful you are.

1. AWARENESS WILL SET YOU FREE

We have already seen how awareness plays a major part in setting you free on your way to becoming an epic creator. Simply reading this principle may have given you a few 'aha' moments as you consciously recognise the voice of your inner critic. It is important to identify and become aware of how it holds you back, which is why giving this inner voice a name really helps. Hence Susan.

Put simply, as soon as we become aware of her, we can tame her. How powerful is that?

Become aware of your inner critic

Simply acknowledging your inner critic is enough to help you return to the real you. This is a useful exercise to get you started:

- Name them.
- When do they tend to get louder?
- What do they usually tell you that you can't do?
- Is there a specific area of your life, like relationships or health, for example, that they tend to pick at when things are going well?

As you go into tomorrow and a few days beyond, be super-aware of your own Self-sabotaging Susan. Take note of when she is at play. When you notice her, in your mind say, 'Thank you, but no thank you.' In other words, give her a polite nod to show that you totally get she is there to protect you, but you don't need that protection at the moment and you will let her know when you do.

2. MAKE THE UNFAMILIAR FAMILIAR AND YOUR HIGHER SELF LOUDER

Our mind is wired to love the familiar and reject the unfamiliar, so when we start to step into our higher self, this sets off Susan's alarm and she panics, doing everything she can to keep us safe. We've seen how she likes what she knows and doesn't like anything unfamiliar. Nice guy? Weight loss? Committed partner? Business success? God no, never had those before – *reject*. But the more you choose the thoughts, beliefs and behaviours of your higher self over Susan's, the stronger and more resilient that part of you becomes – confidently stepping into the spotlight.

I recently found myself in a situation in which my inner critic would have had a field day once upon a time. A painful situation from my past reared its ugly head. I fell into a role I once knew so well: I felt sorry for myself, questioned my worth, indulged in negative thoughts that kept on coming and went into full-blown sabotage mode.

This is normal, by the way, and I am not dissing or shaming myself for the experience. It is part of the healing process to feel the emotions and give yourself space to hurt. When someone does wrong by you, betrays you or disrespects you, you are *allowed* to feel sad. The problem only occurs when we allow ourselves to stay in this trauma and pain for longer than its sell-by date.

For me, this sort of situation would have once shattered me. Instead, I allowed myself to feel it deeply and then, all of a sudden, within just 48 hours, I realised that this was Susan in her glory. In that moment, a beautiful thing happened – I was set free by my awareness of her. I realised that playing the heartbroken girl was a role I subconsciously liked because I was used to it. With that awareness, another even more beautiful thing happened: my higher self stepped in and led us all in another direction. She chose to see this situation as a lesson from the Universe to highlight her growth. Instead of crying on the sofa, she chose to sit down and write the closing pages of this book. She chose happiness and fulfilment over sadness and sorrow. She took back her rightful power and place – and got up to shine.

It is a special moment, when your higher self shows up and takes control of the situation. I realised then that all the work I had done on slowly committing to new thoughts, beliefs and habits had at last made my higher self louder than Self-sabotaging Susan, and that this had happened in the most graceful way, with no shouting required. It was such a subtle energy reversal and reclamation of power – unlike the forceful way Susan shows up when she wants the limelight.

The more you constantly show up in your life with your new behaviours, thoughts, habits and beliefs, the more they will become your familiar everyday norm. The more you nurture your higher self, the more she becomes the leading lady. As you rise up, you will naturally begin to seize on those high-vibe choices, beliefs and behaviours and, when needed, your higher self will come to take your hand and show you the way back to your light.

Your inner critic vs your higher self

Get a piece of paper and make two columns with the headings 'critic me' and 'higher me'. Think of some areas or situations in your life where perhaps your inner critic has been playing the leading role. In one column, list how your inner critic version of you would think or behave in the situation and then, in the other, how your higher self would show up.

Here's an example of how I might address my inner critic if it was stopping me from pursuing a dream of starting a business.

Critic me: Puts off starting my own business out of fear.

· Keeps me stuck in a job I don't really like
· Believes it when people say starting a business is too risky
· Thinks I would fail

Higher me: Starts to take action, even if small just small steps initially, to make it happen.

· Surrounds myself with other people who have launched their own business for inspiration

- Is excited by the challenge and knows the fear can be my fuel
- Ignores people's judgement about starting a business because I know it is their own fears projected onto me

Can you see the difference? It feels more riveting even to read the higher version and quite bizarre to even think we would choose the critic way so often. But you don't need to: you are capable of choosing your higher self's beliefs and actions.

Try it and see how it feels. The awareness alone will be profound but make a commitment to yourself for 24 hours only, to act only in the way your higher self would.

3. GET COMFORTABLE WITH FEELING GOOD

Your ability to manifest is largely rooted in how good you are at feeling good. If you want to attract good things but you don't feel comfortable feeling good, it's not going to work: you are going to resist your manifestations. Coming into alignment with the essence of feeling good is what is going to make you attractive to more good things. Susan doesn't like you feeling that good because when you feel good, you take risks and risks lead you to the unknown, and, remember, her role is to keep you safe. But feeling good is what you deserve.

The sad truth is that many of us have let Susan play the leading role for most of our lives and have therefore forgotten how to feel good about ourselves. In fact, we don't even feel comfortable feeling good. Our addiction to fear, lack and to being the victim, means that even when good things happen, we do everything we can to revert to the patterns, situations and roles that don't serve us but do make us feel safe. We feel weirdly comfortable feeling uncomfortable.

How do we get better at feeling good? Like with any change, we gotta work the muscle. The heavier we lift, the stronger we get. The more you condition your mind to know that this state of happiness is somewhere safe where good things happen, the more it learns that it is the correct behaviour.

High vibes recipe

Below is my recipe for feeling good. It's pretty simple.

1. Do more things that make you feel good – start a new hobby, get creative, dance, sing or read.
2. Spend more time with people who make you feel good.
3. When you don't feel good, don't get angry at yourself – that just creates more negativity.

4. FOCUS ON THE GOOD STUFF

For one day only, commit to avoiding any self-sabotaging behaviours. If you catch yourself doing or thinking something that makes you feel anything but good, bring awareness to it and pick a new thought, a new behaviour.

Just for today, commit to only doing, speaking and surrounding yourself with behaviours, people and experiences that make you feel good. What's the worst that can happen? You can go back to feeling shitty tomorrow? When you realise how good you feel, try to do it for two days at a time, then three days. Before you know it, you won't even have to practise.

Please know that I'm not suggesting you try to be happy all of the time, or that it's possible to achieve round-the-clock contentment. I am not putting any pressure on you at all. Believe it or not, our job here is not to be permanently happy. Emotions are for feeling – every single one of them. The ups and downs are normal. Our goal is not to suppress or shame our unhappiness, it is to work with it to help us move forward and to stop letting it rule our life. It is about accepting that you will feel difficult feelings, while arming yourself with the tools that can help you take your power back. It is about knowing that, at any moment, you have the power to create change in your life for the better.

Every day energy boost

This mantra has become my everyday 'go to'. Whenever I realise I'm being negative, I affirm it until I mean it and feel my energy shift:

'I LOVE to feel good; it feels good to feel good; I am worthy and deserving of feeling good.'

Know What
You Want

You don't need to wait for that thing to arrive to feel good, you can feel good right now.

You might have picked up this book with a very clear idea of what you want to call in to your life. Or perhaps you don't have a clue. You might be more like I was and realise that, on reflection, what you thought you wanted might not be what you really want after all.

The fact is that if you don't know what you want and you aren't communicating it, then you are leaving it up to the Universe to second-guess what to give you. Imagine going to a restaurant and when the waiter asks for your order, you say nothing in reply. Or, worse, you wouldn't order the burger if you wanted pizza, would you?

To get what you want, you gotta truly know what that is and implement ways to express this – and start feeling comfortable asking for it. There is great power in asking for what you want. Sometimes that looks like creating vision boards; sometimes it might be walking along the street and asking the Universe out loud. Yep, I have been known many a time to speak aloud to the Universe about my desires. In fact, I do it all the time.

Here are seven ways to gain more clarity around what it is that you want and how to use that clarity to start declaring your dreams and get creating.

1. GET TO KNOW YOURSELF

In order to know what you truly want from life, you have to get to know yourself better. What makes you tick? What is important to you? What makes you feel loved/joyful/ playful/good? And, of course, what makes you feel the opposite? Knowing these things allows you to implement healthy boundaries and avoid disappointment because you understand yourself well enough to know what you want. One of the best things you can do for yourself is to get to really know yourself.

Who are ya?

Ask yourself the following questions to start to get to know the real you:

- What activities make me feel really good?
- What things/subjects/topics and experiences are important to me?
- What are my strengths and weaknesses as an individual?
- What does a healthy friendship/relationship look like to me?
- What would I like to learn more about or educate myself on further?

2. CREATE THE VISION

If there were no fears or nay-sayers in your way, what is it that you would truly, deeply want? Nobody else is watching or judging you here; there is just you, me and these pages, so you are safe to dream. What do you so deeply desire to call into your life? New job? New partner? You can break this down into areas of your life as well as timescales.

What do you really want?

Take some time to go within yourself and get clear on the experiences, feelings and possessions you want to attract into your life.

Write down what you want to call in or experience in your personal life, your career, your relationships, your health and your wealth within the next six months, year and 2–5 years. Think big here! Now is not the time to play small; do it as though anything is achievable – because it is!

3. BE FREAKING SPECIFIC

If you want the Universe to work with you, it's not enough just to say you want that new job or relationship. If you want to change careers and find one that fulfils you, what does that look like? Do you want more flexible hours, higher pay, more freedom? More everyday opportunities? Be specific. It's in the specificity that the magic happens.

Maybe you want to call in a partner? If you do but you leave it there, you may get a partner who is a total idiot. Trust me when I say specificity is key. Get clear on what that person is like: how do they make you feel? What qualities do they have? What little things do they do that make this your dream relationship? Do you want a partner who is loving, loyal, caring, funny, kind and generous? How do you want to feel around them, what experiences do you want to have together? Remember that if you don't specify, the waiter will pick for you. The more precise you

are, the more information the waiter – aka the Universe –
has to make your dinner as delicious as possible.

4. DIG DEEPER THAN THE SURFACE

As you figure out what you *really* want, clarity on the *real*
reason why you want it is essential. When most people
begin their manifesting journey, they tend to put the usual
things on their wish lists (new cars, big houses, more money,
a relationship). But often there is a deeper reason why we
want these things. Take a moment to consider what energy
lies behind your own wishes. Why do you want that new job?
To feel a sense of status, perhaps? Why do you want a
new relationship? Is it to feel loved? Why do you really
want that new car? So others will admire it and validate
you or because you genuinely like nice cars? Be honest
with yourself.

Remember, if anything that you want is to fill a void or
complete you in some way, that isn't drawing on
manifesting energy. Instead, it's energy that externalises
your happiness and says: 'Only when I get those things,
will I be happy.' We simply cannot manifest from that level.
If your motivation behind your desires comes from a
sense of incompleteness, you are emitting low vibes and
making it far more difficult for yourself. If, when you ask
yourself these questions, you realise that the reasons
behind what you want are because you feel you are
lacking something in your life, that's OK – the next step
will show you what you need to do.

5. HOW WILL IT FEEL?

Here is where the magic really happens. Clarity on the *things* you want in your life is important when it comes to speeding up your manifestations. But clarity on the *feelings* you want to have is essential. Feelings are the activating force behind your manifesting powers. When I did the work on digging deeper into *why* I really wanted the things I wanted, I realised it was because I wanted to *feel* certain things. I was hoping that if I got the things I wanted, then I would feel loved, safe, fulfilled. This is manifesting from lack; this is focusing on what we do not have and thus is not attractive to the things we want. So instead of waiting for our manifestations to 'complete' us and 'make us' feel a certain way, we can do it for ourselves! That way we are going to be attractive to more good things.

When we identify our 'why', we can then focus our energy and attention on where that feeling already *exists* for us and also actively seek *to bring more* of it into our life. For example, if you want a relationship because you want to feel more loved, how can you embody the feelings of love more often in your life? Can you focus on love that already exists with friends or family? Can you bring more of it into your life by loving yourself? Can you watch other people in love and smile, knowing that this is available to you too, instead of feeling bitterness? The moment you fill your life up with love, more loving things are drawn to you!

Life is led by our feelings. Getting into the feeling place when manifesting is like supercharging your manifesting powers and speeds up the process. When you feel it, your mind thinks it already exists, and you become attractive to more. Just a note here: when you realise this, everything changes with what you desire. Yes, I've manifested *things* – the dream career, the flexible working hours, the better bank balance, the lovely house, the great friends. They are all great. But it was all done by focusing on the joy, love, happiness, peace and abundance that already existed in my life and identifying where I could bring in more of these emotions.

6. VISUALISE AND EMBODY IT

So you have got clear and you have got specific – you know what and you know why. *Now you need to feel it, see it, be it.* One of the most powerful tools to attract what you want is visualisation because it helps you to experience the entire essence of what you want to draw in. If you focus all your energy and thoughts on the current reality you have right now, you will only keep getting more of what you already have. It is through visualisation that we can learn to feel, see and embody the person we want to become and the new life we want to attract. The mind loves images and using imagery helps to activate those juicy emotions we want to feel, stimulating them to become the perfect vibrational match for what we want. The more we repeat the visual, the more we firmly create new pathways in our brain and cement those new images and feelings into our subconscious so that we can create new powerful and positive stories that we firmly believe. There are two great ways that you can use visualisation.

Create a vision board: A vision board is a visual representation of all the feelings, experiences and possessions you want to call into your life. By creating a vision board of images that activate your emotions and placing it somewhere you see it every day, you are always mentally rehearsing and embodying the clarity and feelings you want to have. All you need to do is get text that describes what you want and how you want to feel along with pictures of the things you desire and stick these to a board or canvas. Remember to use images and quotes that are focused on the *feeling* and bring out inspiring emotions.

Meditation: This is a powerful way to connect to your higher self and visualise your dream life. When we meditate, we give ourselves the space and opportunity to sit in the present moment, slow down and release our resistant thoughts, withdraw from life's 'to-do lists' and bring peace into our body and soul as we align and connect to our truest self. Being in this space of stillness allows us to get into receiving mode where our creativity can come through and our heart's truest desires can be heard. Adding visualisation to your meditation is a great way to help you imagine and feel your desires while your mind and body are relaxed and free from negative thoughts. Your imagination, affirmations and intentions hold extra power when they have the space and stillness to be truly seen, heard and felt by your subconscious mind.

I have created a guided visualisation meditation that will help you visualise what you really want in life and how it will feel when you have this. You can use it for any specific area in your life or let your imagination run wild and go where it wants to go. (See Resources for more information.) Be playful and indulgent with your imagination; it may feel crazy at first when you start but the more you show up with your new framework, see it, and tell the story, the more you believe it. The power is yours to create what you dream of.

7. GET ASKING!

This is the final and most important part of the puzzle. Ask for your desires. While we are always subtly asking for what we want via our thoughts, feelings and behaviours, we can also simply ask the Universe. I am talking about stating it out loud, writing it down, declaring it, praying for it – whatever feels right for you. But don't skip this last part: let the Universe know you are open to receiving it. I remember being on holiday and realising I had spent ages visualising the kind of partner I wanted – but I hadn't actually asked for it. I went for a walk, put in my AirPods to make it look like I was on the phone rather than talking to myself and started speaking to the Universe! I explained what I wanted this man to look like, how I wanted him to behave and be like in his vibes. Two hours later, he was there in front of me. Exactly as I had described. It was almost laughable. I didn't end up marrying the guy (that *would* be a good story!) but it made me realise how powerful it is when you actually just *ask*. You ask and it is almost instant. However, keep in mind that you only need to ask once. The universe heard you, I promise. Sometimes it does take longer than my example. Try not to get caught up in asking over and over again as this can develop into a desperate energy and can be a sign that what you're asking for is filling a void, rather than generating positive energy.

Change the
Way You Think

You attract what you think about most, the good, the bad and the ugly.

We have seen how our words and thoughts are powerful when it comes to the manifestation of our reality. So our work now is to rewire our everyday thinking to make them as positive as possible.

Where most people go wrong with manifesting is that they try to change their experiences without first changing their thinking and their belief system. The problem with this is that even if we do manage to manifest our desires, they won't stick around because we won't have the support network to keep them in place. If good things come our way, we'll find a way to push them away because, deep down, we still don't believe we are worthy, as we haven't rewired our thoughts and our subconscious mind.

Let me tell you something, no thought is unheard. Even the ones you think were uttered silently, under your breath. The ones you say as a 'joke', thinking they don't count. They do. Your mind hears it all. If you are seeing the world with your Self-sabotaging Susan glasses on and speaking about it and yourself like shit, change won't happen. The manifestation fairies will think you like it like that, so won't sprinkle you with any of the good stuff.

You want to start calling in the juicy, big, high-vibe stuff? Then think and talk juicy. Commit to behaving in new ways, speaking in new ways and seeing things in a new way. The old chat with the 'I am not, I can't. It won't . . .' has got to go. The truth is that you get to choose the thought you have when experiencing something. So our goal is to give more time to the thoughts that leave you feeling happy, positive and excited. Right?

I remember, during a particularly self-neglecting time in my twenties, I was talking to a friend and throwing myself a pity party, sharing how nobody ever gave me compliments. She simply said, 'Honey, when was the last time you gave yourself a compliment?' I knew where she was going with this. I don't think I ever used nice words to describe myself. My daily conversation with myself was mainly focused around how gross I was. I spoke to myself like absolute shit and how I spoke about the world wasn't that different either; I moaned about all the things that were wrong with my life and how stressful everything was. A total joy to be around, I know.

Shortly after that conversation with my friend, I thought I would entertain her theory and started heading to my mirror each morning to tell myself how gorgeously, stunningly beautiful I was. I overdid it of course and at first I felt like a total loser. Susan very quickly followed up with sarcastic comments: 'Ew, that was cringe, you are gross.' It took a while for the practice to feel the slightest bit normal but in time, after many attempts, it became a little less weird and I started to believe it. It wasn't long before people started to really compliment me. Changing the way I thought and spoke about myself and the world changed my reality on so many levels.

You see, when you think about something, you are not just in conversation with yourself, you are telling the Universe what you want. Remember, the catch with thoughts is that the more you think about them, the stronger they become. And you attract what you are thinking about most. If you are constantly thinking about what you do not want, you bring it in. It really is that simple. So we want to make those thoughts and words we use when talking to ourselves as fabulous as we possibly can.

Here is a three-part formula to help you change your inner and outer dialogue, which I call the Rs: Realise, Reframe and Reinforce.

REALISE WHAT YOUR REPEATING THOUGHTS ARE

Start by identifying your most common thoughts about life and yourself and the words you use. Once you are aware, the door opens and you can step through and change the story. Be honest with yourself and take responsibility for the words you have been using, the thoughts you have been thinking.

Be more aware

Here is a great exercise to help you identify your repeating thoughts:

- What do you really think about yourself?
- What thoughts do you regularly have around money, relationships, love, partners, friendships, health, career?
- What is your inner dialogue like with yourself?
- How would you describe yourself?
- What words do you regularly use to talk about things in your life? Do you describe things in a positive way or are you quick to mention the 'problem'?

REFRAME THE THOUGHT AND
CHANGE THE NARRATIVE

Now you've identified your unhelpful thoughts, you need to choose new ones and start changing the narrative around how you see life. Many of the budding entrepreneurs I work with tend to get crippled by fear as they begin to make the changes needed to move into entrepreneurship. When I ask them to share their thoughts and fears around this, it often looks something like this:

· I fear not having a regular income.
· I fear leaving the comfort zone of the 9–5 lifestyle, paid holidays, etc.
· I fear what people will think of me.

What if they chose a different narrative, a completely different perspective? What if 'I fear not having a regular income' became 'I'm excited about having endless earning potential'? Or, 'I fear leaving the comfort zone of the 9–5 lifestyle, paid holidays, etc.' became 'I'm excited about managing my own time, working wherever I want and taking holidays whenever I want.'? How much more exciting and fun is it to say the second statement? You choose how you frame the conversation you have with yourself.

You can do this with anything, not just your fears. You can change your narrative and perspective about everything. What if instead of missing something, you cherished the memory? What if you stopped focusing on how much somebody hurt you and instead considered what you learnt from them? What if you were to reframe your thoughts of 'I'm ugly', 'I'm unloved', 'I'm undeserving' and chose to think 'I am beautiful', 'I'm loved', 'I am fully bloody deserving'?

Reframe the conversation

For any area of your life that you want to improve, ask yourself the questions below:

- How do I talk about this subject and what are my everyday thoughts on it?
- How has this way of thinking and speaking affected my reality? Are there any lessons for me? Can I grow?
- How could I reframe and change the narrative around this to reflect a more positive outlook?

Keep your answers to hand for the next exercise, A Mantra a Day Keeps the Bad Vibes Away, on pages 71-2.

REINFORCE YOUR NEW BELIEFS

Now we need to reinforce these new beliefs so they firmly cement themselves into our programming to replace the old. Repetition is key here: the more we behave, speak, think in a certain way, the more the new story becomes deep rooted. Using more positive words and language in my daily conversation completely changed my vibe and my reality. Think of people in your life who inspire you or who are successful; notice the way that they speak, the words they use. They probably don't often talk about how tough life is, or how stressful and scary it can be. The way they speak – both internally and externally, to themselves and to others – will be about how excited they are, ready they are, interested they are.

As well as images, the second thing your mind responds to is words. Your high vibe is activated by big, bold, fabulous vocab. So make it as spicy as possible. Use exciting, thrilling words, like I am *majorly* excited, I am *super* thrilled, I am *beyond* inspired. The more positive the word, the higher you rise.

A mantra a day keeps the bad vibes away

The most powerful way to use words to help you change not only your energy but your belief system is through affirmations and mantras. Simply put, these are powerfully positive statements that declare your readiness to trust and believe. They can be used to declare how you want to feel, what you want to attract and what you want to tell the world. You can use them to shape the foundation of your day and focus on your plans – and to change your energy at any moment. The idea is that you repeat an affirmation over and over until you believe it, until you feel it. Repeating the words reinforces the belief and energetically helps us to rise, creating more peace, clarity and confidence. Remember to be patient with yourself. It will take time to absorb your new beliefs, so just keep going and you will get there.

Take your Reframe the Conversation answers and create three positive affirmations to reinforce the new beliefs or ways of thinking that you've discovered. To form an affirmation always:

- Use positive language and avoid mentioning the fear/problem.
- Speak in the present tense – as though it already is so.
- Declare your commitment and readiness!

For example, if in the earlier exercise you wrote something like 'I am scared to do something different' your mantra could be 'I am excited for the opportunities that change can bring'. If you hope that a new relationship will help you feel secure and confident, your mantra could be 'I feel safe, secure, and confident in my own skin'.

There is no real way you can go wrong with your affirmations if you use this approach: as long as it feels good for you to say it, you are on! Don't give up after a few tries – repetition is the key!

Repeat your new affirmations daily and jot them on Post-it notes around your house to remind you. Watch your vibration rise!

Let It All Go, Girl

Great things are waiting for you.

We have a wonderful ability as humans to hold on tight to things. Unfortunately, this includes the things that do not serve us and keep us stuck; remember, Susan likes to stay safe. So we cling for dear life to what we know best to ensure that we don't leave ourselves open to hurt or rejection. We like to feel in control. What we don't realise is that when we do this we aren't allowing magic to happen or our new stories to unfold. By holding on to the baggage of the past, we are resisting our growth and all that we desire in our future. Clinging to what you don't want and all that doesn't serve your highest self is exactly what's getting in the way of all you desire. Clinging on to the past will ensure that more of what has happened before will continue to be in your present. We must make space for the new.

For a long time, part of me loved playing the victim. I felt comfy there and knew how to act that role. I was holding on to all the pain, the trauma and the people who'd hurt me. I couldn't let go of this old version of me. Why? Because I was so uncomfortable feeling good and being the higher version of myself.

We often give little time to the shedding and grieving part of the process that must take place as we begin to let go of our old belief systems and identity. A major part of why we block or slow down our manifestations is because we aren't ready to say goodbye to that old version of ourselves and all of the things we have been holding on to so tightly that keep us low vibe. After all, when we've been reliant on them for so many years, it can feel scary, even overwhelming to let go. It isn't necessarily straightforward to create a new reality or a new belief system and commit to your higher self – there is a part of you that must die away and you have to be ready to wave it goodbye.

But if you truly want to grow and call in all the wonderful things you now know you want, then you have to commit to letting go of all of the shit getting in your way. All of it, not just the negative thoughts. In the following pages, we're going to explore some of the things that can hold us back and look at ways to tackle these.

NO MORE SAYING YES WHEN YOU MEAN NO

I used to be queen of the people-pleasing brigade. All in a bid to be liked and loved. Saying yes when every part of me wanted to shout no kept me from manifesting all that I really wanted. You see, saying yes when you mean no confuses the Universe. Every time you settle, you stay stuck. I am talking about jobs, relationships, friendships – all of it. Getting clear on your boundaries and values as an individual is key.

Every time you say yes when you mean yes, you raise your vibe. Every time you say no when you mean no, you raise your vibe and tell the Universe that you mean business and that you aren't f*cking around with the things you don't want. But every time you say yes when you deeply mean no – you lower your vibe. Your self-worth turns down a notch. You tell the world that you don't really want the thing you just said you wanted. Remember our lovely waiter? If you ordered salmon and he brought you chicken would you accept it? If so, did you really want salmon at all?

Know your non-negotiables. What things you are willing to put up with and what won't you accept? Look at each area of your life in turn and identify what your core values are. What behaviours do you or don't you tolerate? When you know this, it is a lot easier to be able to communicate your values, spot the red flags when they appear and put your boundaries in place.

Please note, there is no right or wrong here – this must be personal to you. You may, for example, be a single parent and a non-negotiable for you is that your new partner has to want to play a role in helping you bring up your child. Or you may want a new job and a non-negotiable for you is that you must be able to leave work by 5pm to get home to your family. However, you may tolerate working late one day a week.

Gaining clarity on your non-negotiables and what you are willing to tolerate is imperative when it comes to building a life you love. This knowledge will help you make better decisions, communicate your needs and accept what you truly want, while saying no to the things that do not fit with your own personal desires and needs.

WHAT ARE YOUR NON-NEGOTIABLES?

Take each area of your life, such as relationships, career and free time, and make a list with headings like the following:

Relationships

Important to me:
Not willing to tolerate:
Is negotiable:

Fill this in to get clear on your non-negotiables and what you will accept.

Just to be clear, you don't have to justify saying no or apologise for that to anyone else. Establish your boundaries with love and kindness without apologising for prioritising yourself and your values.

YOUR BODY KNOWS

When you are asked to do something you don't want to do or you find yourself in a situation that does not serve your highest good, your body always knows. Check in with yourself next time you find yourself about to say yes even though it feels icky. Close your eyes, feel into your body and sense if the answer really is yes or if you are really just people-pleasing. If it isn't a full-body, all-over 'F*ck yes!' then it is a no.

Here are some questions to ask yourself to check in with your boundaries:

- Where in my life am I settling for what is not a full-body yes?
- In which areas am I settling for half-assed versions of what I really want?
- Are there things I am doing that don't match up with what I have said I want?
- Do I have the emotional and physical capacity right now to do what is being asked of me?
- Is this situation in line with my desires?
- Do I feel comfortable with the idea of doing this?
- Is this a yes or am I doing it to be liked?

LET GO OF PAIN, ANGER AND TRAUMA

It is time, my love, to let go of all of that hate, anger, resentment and pain you have been holding on to. I know how deeply you were wounded and how it left you vulnerable, scared and sad. I do – trust me, I do. But it isn't going to serve your higher self. I felt scared for years to let these feelings go but it changed my life when I did.

Forgiveness: This really will set you free. I know it is the most irritating thing to hear. But it is true. It is only yourself you are punishing by not forgiving those who've hurt you – and that includes the hurt you've caused yourself. Forgiveness is the antidote to hate. You are saving yourself, not anyone else, when you forgive.

Declare it: Write down on a piece of paper all of the painful things that you are committing to letting go of and burn it. Burn it and let it go in your mind as it burns.

RELEASE THE HURT

Here are some cues to help you declare your readiness to let go of pain and practise forgiveness:

- · What negative situations are you letting go of?
- · What things are you familiar with that you want to make unfamiliar?
- · What self-defeating behaviours are you going to put a stop to?
- · What situations are you going to say no to?
- · Where can you forgive yourself?

- Who can you forgive?
- What pain are you holding on to, that it is time to let go of?

Something magic happens when we let go and let be – we allow things to become possible for us, beyond anything we can imagine.

LET GO OF THE NEED TO CONTROL

We love to make things go our way. We spend so much time overthinking, pre-empting and micromanaging the way things work out or, worse, *might* work out. But when we try to control absolutely every eventuality, we don't leave any room for magic to happen. For random, unexpected greatness to take place. Really, all we are doing when we try to control everything is to suffocate it with our energy. We are repelling what we want because we become a match for low-vibe things. When we are obsessed with controlling an outcome, we are driven by fear and worry around something *not happening* instead of allowing something even better than we could have ever expected to occur.

One of the BIGGEST secrets to manifesting is that you gotta let go of the need to figure out the hows, whos, whats, and whys – and just let the Universe bring you the goods you've asked for. Your job is not to control; your job is to get clear on what you want and to live in alignment with your highest vibration. When you are there, you can let go, knowing you are the perfect vibrational match for all that you want. You can trust the Universe to deal with the how.

Get Good at Seeing the Good

You cannot manifest what you desire if you spend all your energy focusing on the absence of it.

When we are thinking about what we want, it is too easy fall into a pattern of focusing too much on what we actually *don't want* or *don't have*. How often have you wanted something but instead of thinking how lovely it will feel to have it, you think about how unhappy you are that you don't have it yet or how disappointing the version of it you do have is? Or panic that you may never get it? It is so common to give all of our energy to the problem instead of the desired outcome. You want a new job, for example, but you want one because you hate how boring and energy draining your current job is. This is normal and I see it all the time. Focusing all of your energy on how much you hate your current job won't get you that shiny new role. Refocus your attention into wanting a new job because you are excited about thriving in a new environment and thrilled at the prospect of new challenges – that will get you the new job. Your energy and attention will then be reflecting the feelings and emotions you want, not what you currently dislike.

Remember, the Universe is always listening and you are always manifesting. Imagine that you desperately want to call in a loving relationship, yet whenever you mention a potential partner you tell everyone that you are hopeless in love and that relationships are stressful and end up in heartbreak. Guess what? You are focusing all of your energy and thoughts on what you do not have, what isn't there, what isn't available to you. What are you telling the Universe? Please don't send me my ideal partner; relationships are too stressful!

Our goal when manifesting is to act as though we already have what we want. That approach will get us into the vibration of manifesting our desires. Here is the thing:

- You cannot create a healthy body when your focus is on how much you hate your body.
- You cannot become wealthy from always talking about how little money you have.
- You cannot call in a dream job that fulfils you when you are focused on how much you hate your current job.
- You cannot attract the right partner when you feel like you always end up with the wrong person.
- You cannot call in happiness when all of your attention is given to the problems in your life.

In other words, you can't manifest something you desire if you spend all of your time and energy focusing on the absence of it. What you focus on, expands. So we want to give more time and energy to the good things and feeling good.

HOW TO FEEL GREAT AND ATTRACT WHAT YOU WANT

Below is my FEEL GREAT formula – a step-by-step guide to how to devote more energy to the good in your life and take responsibility for where you are placing your energy, so you become attractive to the things you want.

F – FEEL THE EXCITEMENT!

Instead of focusing on the problems, can you turn your attention to how EXCITED you are for your desired outcome and all the other wonderful things in your life? Finding joy in all that you do is one of the greatest ways to get what you want in life. When you turn to excitement instead of fear and focus on all the exciting things that may come your way, you will be a vibrational match for all that you dream of.

E – EMBODY IT AS THOUGH IT ALREADY IS!

Imagine knowing that you don't have to wait for what you want to feel a certain way! Yep, when you understand the essence of why you want what you want, you can choose to feel as though it is already here! If you want a relationship in your life, can you behave like you already have it? What would you be doing? How would you be feeling? Acting as though your desired reality is already your current reality is a powerful tool to manifesting what you want. You may feel silly at first but who is watching? When starting my entrepreneurial journey, I blocked out my calendar with a busy waitlisted schedule – and two months later, I had a waitlist. This stuff works – trust me!

E – ENVIRONMENT ALIGNMENT IS ESSENTIAL

Aligning your environment with what you want and what makes you feel good is essential to protecting your energy. Surround yourself with people who light you up and have shared goals and visions, and fill your social feeds with individuals who make you feel good or inspired. Taking pride in your environment and appearance sets the tone for how good you feel and, thus, what you are able to manifest.

I see it every single day within my communities. When women join our courses, they make lifelong friends with people they might never have connected with otherwise and because these women have a shared vision, values and goals, magic goes down. Take responsibility for what is contaminating your own energy field and limit your exposure to it.

L – LOOK AT THE NOW

Being more present is an instant drug for joy. When you are worrying about potential problems in the future and anticipating what is next, you are embodying a low fear vibe. When you are always searching for problems, you create more problems. When you are fixated on all that went wrong in the past, you are missing the joy now. The now is all we have, guys – the past has gone, the future is not here, but this moment that you are in right now is yours – so why waste it thinking about what wasn't or what could be?

G – GRATITUDE IS YOUR NEW BFF

Being grateful for what you already have is the greatest recipe for calling in more good stuff and giving up all that you think you need. It can be so easy to overlook the little things that make you smile. Whatever your situation, there will be great things going on; there will always be something good to focus on. Go there, focus on it, appreciate everything you are grateful for and ensure that you are giving more attention to those things than to all that is missing.

Gratitude practice

Before my feet even touch the ground in the morning, I say what I am excited about in the day ahead and when I go to bed, I give thanks for what went well that day. You can do the same, it takes just a few moments.

Try it now just to see how it feels. Mentally note, or write them down if you wish, all of the things (include the small ones) that you are grateful for today, in this moment. Did something go well for you? Are you grateful for the home that you live in? The friend that did something nice?

When we focus our energy and attention on gratitude, we instantly raise our vibration.

R – REMOVE THE 'SHOULD' AND DROP THE EXPECTATIONS

Getting clear on what you want and what your values and boundaries are is great, sure. But expecting others to behave in a certain way gives away your power and is a recipe for disappointment. We may tolerate and not tolerate certain behaviours but remember that the power stays with you: you are the artist of your painting, so keep hold of the paintbrush and don't allow others to make you feel a certain way if they don't meet you at your high levels. Living life on a 'all that should have been done' level limits your manifesting powers because it is focused on what is missing and places conditions on your happiness. No person, thing or outcome should be the reason for your happiness. It may add to it, but not be the source ot it – you can do that for yourself. By letting go of expectations, we give ourselves the opportunity and permission to accept our reality. When we break free from expecting people to behave a certain way, we can begin to enjoy them for who they are.

This also applies for you too, my love: quit placing such high expectations on yourself of how you 'should' be performing, how your life 'should' look or what you 'should' be doing and let yourself be as you are.

E – EMPHASISE THE WINS

When was the last time you gave yourself a pat on the back? We can become so caught up in wanting more that when a goal is achieved, we forget that the milestone we just passed was one we once dreamt about reaching. Celebrating the wins is an instant way to feel good and protect your energy. When we truly celebrate ourselves and the world, we let go of fears and worries about what is missing and break free from lack-based living.

At the end of every week, I check in and note down all of the victories – big, small and teeny tiny – I had that week. Don't overlook the smallest things, they are often what allows the bigger things to happen.

A – AVOID THE DRAMA AND JUDGEMENT OF GOSSIP

I was once partial to a glass of rosé and a gossip, but while the conversation was entertaining, I was always left feeling icky. Deciding to stop dropping judgement on others and myself while removing myself from gossip was one of the best things I did. I didn't even realise how much time and energy I'd been devoting to the drama of gossip. It felt like that was normal behaviour. It isn't. Not when you surround yourself with the right people, anyway. When I started to take responsibility for my energy, I began taking myself away from conversations that involved judgement, drama and gossip, and I instantly noticed how much better I felt. Even if you are not involved in gossip, surrounding yourself with it is enough to knock your vibration.

T – TRUST THAT YOU ARE EXACTLY WHERE YOU ARE MEANT TO BE

A magical thing happens to our energy when we simply trust that our life as we know it is all in perfect timing and as it is meant to be. When we can trust in this, we find peace. I discovered this for myself when I gave up trying to figure it all out and started letting the Universe do its thing.

Trust It All

You are *always* being supported.

Let's be honest, the hardest part when you want something is the waiting. *Is it really coming? How can I make it come quicker? Should I visualise more? Did I tell the Universe loud enough? Did I specify well enough?* All we are doing here is distrusting, blocking and getting in the way.

Trust that the Universe heard and is working to make it happen – if it is the right thing for you and the time is right. This is the hardest step but the most important. If you truly want your desires to happen quickly, you have to start embodying more trust in your life and in yourself.

One of the major blocks to manifesting our desires is not trusting that they are on their way. It is our lack of trust that causes us to overwork, overthink and people-please. It keeps us stuck in jobs, relationships and situations that don't serve us – because we don't believe that there is anything better out there. When we are living out of alignment with trust, we live in a world of anxiety, indecision, confusion and fear, and thus we block the Universe from giving us the very things we said we want. When we learn to trust, we sit in a place of peace, knowing that our desires are on their way. And when we celebrate the synchronicities, the world keeps sending us more.

Here are four ways to cultivate more trust in your life.

1. LOOK FOR THE WINKS

I know it doesn't always feel like you are being guided and you might not think miracles exist, but they do when you believe in them. They are happening all around you; every single day the Universe is giving you signs. I call them 'winks' from the Universe. Some of the biggest decisions in my life were based on whether I'd seen a butterfly or not. Sounds crazy I know, but it is mine and the Universe's little way of talking to each other to let each other know that all is OK. I ask for the butterfly to appear whenever I am in need of clarity or direction or sometimes I just see one when I am in a place that feels great. It is my little wink from the Universe that I am on the right track and being supported. At every pivotal moment in my life, a butterfly has been around. As I sit here right now, there is a little girl outside flying a butterfly kite. It is one of the most magical things when you get that nod that you are in the right place.

Some of you will be thinking that you don't get signs but that's because you are just not seeing them. The Universe is always finding ways to give you messages, signs and winks to guide you. When you open up to the possibilities of seeing them, you get winked at a little more.

How to find and use your sign

Close your eyes and draw your attention to your heart. Ask: 'What is my sign?' It could be a number, an animal, a feather, anything! If it doesn't come to you, don't worry or overthink it. Simply ask the Universe to show you your sign in the next few days, let go, trust and then pretty much forget about it. You will know when you see it. You may even have more than one sign. Besides a butterfly, I have the number 11 and I also take it as a sign when I see feathers.

There is no right or wrong way to work with your sign. I sometimes have a decision to make and ask the Universe to show me a butterfly if it is the right one. Sometimes I just ask the Universe to show me that I am supported and I see one. Whenever a butterfly appears, I give it a little nod, smile to myself or tell a friend so that the Universe hears me celebrate it.

Not seeing a sign is also a major indicator. If you are in a situation that you know is not serving you and you ask for a sign and you don't get it, the Universe is telling you, 'Nope, honey, not this time!' The key part here is getting into conversation with the Universe. Speak to it, it is always listening.

A client from my RISE programme messaged me as I was writing this chapter to tell me when she was doing the work for one of the month's modules, she screamed for the Universe to show her what her sign was and, within seconds, a meaningful place that she had always been drawn to appeared as a picture in her Google search. It works pretty quick when you ask!

2. YOU ARE ALWAYS SUPPORTED

Signs can come in other forms, too, such as what I call 'nudges'. There have been times in my life when I honestly felt like the world was against me. Now I realise that what felt like massive F-Us from the Universe were actually its way of showing me that change needed to happen, that I wasn't on my destined path and I wasn't listening. It was wholeheartedly supporting me and showing me a new way.

The moments that feel like massive bitch slaps from the Universe are its way of holding you up, giving you the nudge to move in the right direction or showing you what you needed to see. Whether it feels like it or not, it is always on your side, helping you shine brighter, grow taller, rise higher. It is dedicated to helping you tune back into your power, quit settling and lead the life you deserve by helping you evolve and go where you are meant to go. I know when you're on your knees it feels hard to believe this, but I promise you, one day you will see it.

When the Universe knocks you off your feet, trust that there is always a reason why. When faced with a problem, we can always instantly feel like the world is against us. What if instead we looked for the lesson to be learnt, the growth to unlock, the place unhealed to heal?

These two things, when I am in the midst of a problem, help me to relax and trust:

1. Everyone is a teacher.
2. Problems are pathways to greater things.

Once, the Universe had to send me a pretty big nudge to make me listen and it turned into one of my greatest moments of growth. I was juggling two areas of work and kept putting off the decision about which one was going to be my full-time occupation. I kept myself busy from 6am to 2am every day so I never had to face the issues I was ignoring. Until one day, I was exercising and fell off some monkey bars, landing on my back. I was literally knocked off my feet. For six weeks, I wasn't able to exercise or work. I couldn't do anything other than be with my thoughts and face all the decisions I was putting off and focus on the personal healing that I needed long before the accident. In this space, I took the steps needed to begin my own business, which my heart desperately wanted and which led me to exactly where I am right now. The Universe had been sending me nudges, little nods and niggles that I was overdoing it. But I wasn't listening, so it had no option but to make me listen by knocking me off my feet.

In any situation, there is always light to be found in the darkness. In fact, we cannot turn on the light if there is no darkness there before. What if you knew that always? Would it mean you never worried about the things that could go wrong, knowing that even problems can lead to growth, healing or a better direction? Every moment of sadness in your life, every single obstacle you have faced and each tear you have cried shaped who you are right now. It taught you a lesson, helped you grow, led you to a certain path and, more importantly, it happened to you because the divine Universe wanted it to.

Think of times in your life where you felt unsupported, let down, challenged. Ask yourself, did this lead you in a different direction? To a better place? Next time you are faced with a challenge, or if there is a problem troubling you now, can you look at it from a different perspective and see where the growth lies? What lessons could be learnt? What good can you make out of it?

3. DROP THE FANTASY TIMELINE

One pivotal part to the manifestation game is to know that time is always on your side and all will happen exactly when it is meant to. Whenever I host a Q+A, whether it be online or in a masterclass, the questions usually start the same way: 'I'm 24 and have never . . .' 'I am now 31 but . . .'

'I am 40, so . . .' It's as though the questioner's age has a part to play in why something hasn't happened for them. Like time is running out or there is some sort of timeline we must follow to be 'on track'.

Believe it or not, there is no predestined schedule that determines when we should marry, buy a home or enjoy career success. It doesn't exist.

When you feel like your manifestations aren't coming, yet you've done all the 'work' and changed your beliefs, it might be as simple as it just isn't your time yet. There are still things in my life that I desire that I have not manifested yet and I have days where I get impatient and slip back into my old low-vibe thinking. However, when I truly connect, I fall into a deep sense of trust that those things will happen at the perfect moment – and not a minute sooner.

Sometimes, the things we want simply aren't meant for us right now. This doesn't mean your manifesting game isn't strong, it just means you're not ready for your desired outcome yet, or it isn't ready for you. Yep, it may not be about you at all; maybe that thing is just getting itself ready for you! Keep the faith that it is coming. One of the greatest superpowers when it comes to manifesting is letting go and trusting that your desires are being heard, and they will be on their way when the time is right.

4. TRUST THAT YOUR DESIRES ARE ON THEIR WAY!

I often get asked if it is possible to manifest too much and overdo it, and yes, it is. The mistake many make with their manifestations is that they get busy doing all the 'work' – almost too busy! Believe it or not, the more you force your manifestations and fixate on what you want, the more you can push them away. When we really want something, we usually become very attached to the idea of it. However, that slows down the manifesting process because our desperation causes us to emit a low vibration. Ever noticed how the things you could live without tend to manifest quicker than the things you really, really want? They feel like they take forever, right? If we are desperate for an outcome or obsessed with manifesting it, we are essentially driven from a place of fear and lack. We are telling the Universe that we don't trust it will make things happen for us.

If you need someone to say they love you, or you need your boss to tell you that you are amazing, or you grow desperate for new clients in your business, you are emitting low vibrations. Others are going to feel energetically restricted by you. They will subconsciously resist you because nobody wants to be controlled. I see it all the time with my clients: their desperation for a particular outcome is exactly what is getting in the way of them having it.

The more you can learn to detach patiently from your desires, knowing that they are being looked after as long as you embrace your higher vibrations, the quicker you will receive what you want. I can't tell you how many times I have got clear on something I want, visualised it, affirmed it, got comfy feeling it and popped it on my vision board – and then panicked and fixated on it if it didn't arrive within five minutes. Of course it never arrived because I was in a state of lack and fear, worrying about it. It is almost always the things that I've nearly forgotten about that appear exactly as I want them to a few months or sometimes a year down the line. It's the simple detachment that makes it happen.

Check in with your desires: are you fixated on them? Thinking about them every single day? Are you driven by fear and disbelief about them coming into your life or have you surrendered to trust that they are on their way?

Trust that the Universe has heard you. What is meant for you will not miss you. What you went through, helped you grow stronger. People will walk into your life exactly when they are meant to and leave when they should. Your desires are on their way. Sit back and enjoy the ride.

Mantras for trusting the universe

Here are some mantras to help you cultivate trust. Say them over and over. Write them on Post-it notes and place them around your house where they will catch your eye.

- · I trust that I am on the right path and that all is happening exactly as it should.
- · I know that it is safe to let go and let life unfold as it is meant to. That with surrendering comes peace.
- · I realise that controlling and pushing means blocking and resisting guidance. Instead, I choose trust.
- · I trust that I am always supported, held and looked after and that all that is meant for me will not pass me.
- · The more I let go, the higher I rise.

No More
Playing Small

If you want to call in big things, you gotta put fear to bed.

Everything great that I've achieved came from stepping out of my comfort zone and doing something that required me to break through my fears and to feel somewhat like an imposter. The fear of feeling like an imposter crippled me for a long time: I avoided doing things I wanted to do because I felt inadequate. But when I learnt of the greatness that awaits on the other side of our comfort zones, I realised that, actually, feeling like an imposter is a gift. If you don't ever feel like an imposter in your life, you aren't scratching the surface of what you are capable of achieving. If you aren't pushing the boundaries in some form, wondering who the hell you are to be doing what you are doing, or wondering if you truly have what it takes, then you are playing small – and playing small means you live a small life.

Fear alone is powerful enough to hold you back from having all that you want. It really is simple: a fear-based life will ensure you stay disconnected from your power. It might feel comfy there, free from risk, ridicule and rejection, but, let's be honest, it is actually rather uncomfortably comfy, right? Nothing really feels that great, rewarding or exciting inside our comfort zone.

When we are living in fear, we feel anxious, worried and negative. I am not talking about healthy fears, like those that we need to help us detect dangerous situations and protect ourselves and our loved ones. I am talking about irrational, unreasonable fears that are often focused on the 'what if's' and concerned with all the things that *could* go wrong. These fears are rooted in imagination and fantasy, which is why lots of psychologists like to say that fear stands for Fantasised Experiences Appearing Real – it is all based on what we *think* may happen, not what actually will happen.

HOW FEAR BLOCKS YOUR
MANIFESTING ABILITIES

Fear is a huge factor in all of the unfulfilled dreams out there in the world and one of the biggest blocks to our manifestations. Not only is it a low-vibe emotion – and we know low-vibe emotions attract low-vibe living – it is a total illusion that *we created*. We are so focused on all that could go wrong that we manifest this into our reality.

Fear also affects our behaviour and actions. It can overwhelm and cripple us to the point where it leads to inaction, keeping us stifled and constricted, causing us to stay firmly where we are. When we are too scared to make a move or take action, our outcomes remain the same; whereas actions equal results. When there is no action, there cannot be any results.

Sometimes, however, fear can cause us to take the wrong sort of action in our panic that disaster may strike if we do not do something. For example, we may have such a deep-rooted fear of not being able to pay the bills that we say yes to work that we do not have enough time, energy or capacity to do, or that isn't authentic to our truth, because we are in *desperate need* of that extra income. This is fear-based action, rooted in lack, and not the expansive thoughts and feelings of excitement and possibility that will help us manifest.

The good news? Our thoughts and the images we see are the source of the fears we allow to manifest – and who controls our thoughts? Us! We have the power to change them by choosing thoughts that are full of love, not fear.

But what if we actually started to cherish our fears a little more? What if it was right there in our fears that we saw the truth about the places we wanted to go, the things we dreamt of? What if we became excited about our fears because within them lie our truest desires? What if we turned around our thinking and instead of letting our fears cripple us, we turned them into fuel . . . ?

WHAT ARE YOU REALLY AFRAID OF?

How many times has fear got in the way for you? Held you back from applying for that dream job or telling someone how you feel? Going for that promotion or starting your side hustle? Or simply speaking your truth? And what is this really about? Is it the fear of judgement? Fear of failure? Fear of being too much? Fear of not being good enough? Fear that someone else may do it better? That you may look silly, or the feeling may not be mutual? Which is it for you? Or is it all of it? Be honest with yourself. How often do you let fear win? And where has that truly got you?

Here's a theory for you: the fear of not being enough or being too much – are they both the same fear? Is this really just being afraid of being yourself? Being the you that you haven't truly gotten to know because you have spent much of your life being whoever everyone else wants you to be or behaving how life tells you that you should. Are you really petrified of being totally raw, the authentic you? Is this about fear of your most powerful, risen self?

And as for that fear of failure, rejection and ridicule you have – what if failure actually didn't exist? Or, what if people aren't actually talking about you because they are too focused on their own insecurities? What if this was just an excuse you made because, really, you are immensely afraid of just how powerful you are?

When I think back to all the things I didn't do because I let fear win, I can see that I never really questioned my ability to achieve most of them. No, I always knew I had what it took. The issue was my fear of how magical and powerful I could be; my self-worth wasn't strong enough yet for me to know how to be that successful person or to feel like I deserved to succeed. I let myself believe that it was my fear of what other people might say so that I could blame everyone else for why I didn't start.

I truly believe that most of us are scared of how deep our love goes, how powerful our anger can be. Of how successful we can be and how much we can give. I think we are afraid of our power because we think it might frighten others, frighten ourselves. Because all our lives we have been told to dim our light.

But by staying safe in that comfort zone, letting those fears win, what are you missing out on?

- What would life look like for you if you knew absolutely no one would judge you?
- What would life feel like if you were doing everything you loved?
- What would you do if money was no issue?

- What would it feel like not to worry about what others think of you?
- What would you do if you really believed in your superpowers?

If you are letting fear win, you are keeping yourself small. Keeping yourself small means staying in lack and from lack, remember, we cannot manifest. From fear, we cannot manifest. When thinking about the things you want to call into your life, remember to take note of whether or not there is fear-based energy behind your desires.

So how can we overcome our fears?

KNOW THAT FAILURE DOES NOT EXIST

I truly do not believe failure exists. Not when you think about it. What is your definition of failure? Where did it come from? Your parents? Friends? The TV? Or did it come from you? For me, failure only exists if you believe in it. It is us who sets the bar of what we deem to be failure or success – so what if you changed the benchmark?

Imagine you want to start a new business but you're worried it might fail if not enough people buy the first collection. You count less than ten sales to be a failure. Your friend does the exact same thing but her definition of 'failure' is less than five sales. She sells eight items and is over the moon about her success. You sell eight and are disappointed you sold less than your target. Who is going to thrive? Whose definition of failure or success was correct? Nobody's. You created the problem.

Failure is what you define as failure. Failure is when you don't do anything. When you do not start.

For me, failure is when you don't do anything at all. I have had countless perceived 'failures' in my entrepreneurial life – and you know what? Every single one of them now makes perfect sense and had to happen to get me here. Nothing is a failure when you see everything as a lesson.

IF SOMEONE IS JUDGING YOU, IT'S REALLY ABOUT THEM

The biggest fear for most of the women I work with is of what others might think or say about them. There's this overwhelming fear that our 'friends', family, colleagues and community will ridicule, judge and shame us for shining bright. For stepping into our power and being confident enough to make our dreams happen when they can't.

Read that again: *when they can't*. Truth is, what we judge in others often relates to the unhealed places in ourselves. People who have something to say about what you are or aren't doing are usually resentful about what they aren't achieving themselves. That said, much of our fear around what others might say is completely illusory anyway. Most people are so concerned with their own stuff that they don't have time to worry about yours. You will never be criticised by someone doing more than you, only by those doing less.

Who are you trying to be enough for? Why does it matter what they *might* say? The only person you need to be enough for is you. The only person's approval you need is yours.

WHAT'S THE WORST THAT CAN HAPPEN?

Whatever your deepest fears, what is the worst that can happen if you go for them? If you tell someone you like them and they don't reciprocate, what do you lose? And what if you never told them because you let fear win, while they were also too afraid to tell you what they felt? Then you both miss out. We think we have so much to lose by going for it, when, in reality, we give up far more by playing safe. Staying in that comfort zone will attract the same old low-vibe stuff over and over again.

When I was working myself up to leave my full-time career to start my business, asking myself what was the worst that could happen was what gave me the strength to change. I realised my worst-case scenario was not being able to afford my rent and moving back into my mum's for a bit while she cooked me dinner and washed my pants as I found a new job – so not that bad . . . I get it, everyone's worst case scenario is different – but is it really that terrible?

GET COMFORTABLE WITH DISCOMFORT

Doing more things outside of your comfort zone, no matter how small they are, will lead to greater things. Remember, your mind is wired to cling on to the familiar. So the answer is to make new behaviours outside of that safe place your new norm. Take baby steps at first: walk a different way to work, read a new book, speak your truth a little more. Small changes make up the bigger picture and will make the big leaps feel less daunting.

I challenge you to do one thing every single day that scares you in some way. You will find that in a year's time, the things that once crippled you with fear will no longer have a leg to stand on.

If you keep letting fear stop you, you will never lead a fulfilled life – a life where you achieve all of those things you think about. Do you want to keep watching people do what you want to, live the life you want to live? Have the things you want to have? *Or do you want to go get it?* Playing small is not serving anyone, least of all you.

REFRAME YOUR FEARS

Consider the following to help you reframe your fears:

- · What are your fears?
- · How are they serving you?
- · What have they held you back from?
- · What would you be doing if you didn't have them?
- · How can you reframe them into a positive statement?
- · What is the worst that can happen?

Make Room for
the Good Stuff

It is in stillness and silence that we can connect to our power.

It might sound counterproductive to say you need to slow down to speed up your manifestations, but believe it or not, we do not get our wants quicker the faster we go – and certainly not when there isn't room for these to come in. When we slow down, a number of things happen that support our manifesting power:

- We can hear the guiding voice of our intuition and are able to connect to our power.
- We make space for our desires to land.
- We emit a relaxed energy that we trust our desires are on their way.
- We create room for creativity and change.

Slowing our pace makes space for the faster vibrations to come in. Before I slowed mine, I was constantly stuck in lower vibrational feelings of fear, anxiousness and worry. I felt as though I was always in a rush to get everything done. Rushing is a sign of fear and disbelief – and so is keeping yourself busy. When you rush, you are telling the Universe that you don't trust it to bring you your desires and that you do not believe anything will happen for you unless you get it done quickly, by yourself.

We have this deep-rooted belief that we only get more when we do more, but that couldn't be further from the truth. Far more greatness, success, joy and happiness has come into my life through slowing down, taking my time and creating space. When we live our lives in a full-on, intense way, we leave no room for the seeds that we have planted to grow or for the Universe to get in.

Living at a slower pace means you emit the energy that says you know all is being looked after, that you are fully, deeply and wholeheartedly in trust. It allows you to take action aligned with your truest desires and values, not forced or based on fear of what could go wrong. It also gives you the room to hear your intuition.

MASTER THE ART OF RECEIVING

When we slow down, we make space for the bread to rise, the plane to land, the flower to bloom, the light to shine. While it is important to get clear on what you want – embodying the feeling, visualising it and asking for it – if there is no space for it to land, it will keep circling above you. I mean, if you want a relationship in your life but have no time to even grab yourself a glass of water, how will you nurture a full-on other human being in a relationship? Clear the calendars, make space in the cupboards, open the blocks around your heart and get into a readiness state of receiving as though it is already there. By now, you are hopefully on the way to believing you are worthy of receiving, so create the space for it.

HEAR YOUR INTUITION AND ACCESS YOUR CREATIVITY

We live in a noisy world where the word 'busy' is often used as a badge of honour. For years, silence rarely existed in my life and I would avoid it at all costs to ensure I didn't have to face the thoughts and fears I was hiding from, or the creative ideas that would require me to step up and make change. So I kept the noise on all the time to avoid it all. Even when I was working, I wouldn't give myself space to come up for air. And it was all a distraction from my higher self and a subconscious decision to avoid my greatness and remain disconnected from my power.

I had this feeling of anxiety all the time – a burning feeling that desperately wanted to get some air time. Now when I feel anxious, I create space, connect to my creativity and I am relieved almost instantly. It was my power all along, trying to get out.

Your power is accessed in silence. Your intuition, creativity and greatness are accessed in silence. The answers you seek will only come when there is silence. Every idea, great thought, answer I have ever needed has come from myself – in silence.

Your intuition is one of your greatest powers. It is the part of you that knows the truth and tells you when something is not quite right, that you need to explore or change directions. Your intuition will always guide you to growth, to the truth and your purpose in life. The problem isn't that some of us do not have good intuition, it's that we do everything we can to avoid it by keeping busy. Your intuition is one of your most reliable sources, so be bold and brave enough to slow down and listen to it. Even if it tells you something you do not want to hear.

There are solutions to your problems that can only be provided by you; there are questions about your life decisions that only you can answer. Within you is all the wisdom you need. I promise you, there is a part of you that knows exactly what to do, what the next step is and what the decision needs to be. You just aren't creating the space to listen. We cannot connect to the intuitive part of ourselves and our power if we avoid silence.

HOW TO ACCESS YOUR MOST ALIGNED STATE

You have heard me use the word 'alignment' a number of times in this book. All this means is to be in coordination, in proper working order. It is when we come into alignment that we are able to rise up the vibrational levels and, thus, connect to our power. Coming into alignment is an essential part of your ability to manifest.

Learning which activities help me come into alignment, and to feel more calm, peaceful and conscious, has been pivotal in enabling me to harness my potential and power. It took a while to identify what works for me but nature walks, journaling, meditating and listening to soulful music are just a few of the things that help me reconnect.

Are there certain times or activities that make you feel most aligned, at peace and connected to your power?

WHAT ALIGNS YOU WITH YOUR POWER?

To establish what will help you connect to your power, ask yourself the following questions:

- · When do you feel completely at ease, peace and connected?
- · What activities leave you feeling calm and joyful?

- What can you do for ages that never feels like a chore?
- What comes naturally to you and makes you feel free?
- When do you feel most calm and connected?
- Have there been any activities that you have done which have given you great clarity, direction or ideas?

When we understand what being in alignment means for us and match that with the clarity we have around what we want to create and call into our lives, we can take aligned action. This is action that is in pursuit of our desires, yet free from fear or the need to manipulate an outcome. Once we have practised bringing ourselves into alignment and feel connected, we can then take action in every area of our life, knowing that this comes from guidance and passion rather than grind and force. You will know when an action is aligned as you enjoy the process, it feels easy and just seems to flow. When we learn to take compelled, inspired, aligned action, this is when our greatest manifestations take place.

A word on actions. It is important to ensure you are moving in the direction of your desires by taking action. We can't just sit back and expect it all to fall on our laps. You need to make moves to show the universe you are serious about what you want. If you are saying you want one thing but accepting half-assed versions, settling for less, you are telling the universe that you don't really want what you said you wanted. So be sure to be aware that your everyday actions match up with what you say you want.

Here are some ways in which you can bring more downtime into your life to help you connect and align to your power.

SET THE PACE WITH A SLOWER, HIGH-VIBE START

The way you start your day sets the vibrational tone for the hours to come. Immersing yourself in a morning routine with high-vibe activities will have you walking out of the door with an energy that attracts all. Instead of grabbing your phone first thing, can you write a gratitude list and say your daily mantras out loud? Can you put on some high-vibe music instead of the low-vibe news? Can you allow yourself time to organise your day, your house and your world before you run out the door? Sometimes, just having the time to sip a coffee and eat some cereal in your pjs is ultimate bliss.

Here are some high-vibe suggestions for your morning routine:

- Listening to your favourite music
- Reading or listening to a book that makes you feel good
- Dancing or practising yoga
- Saying your daily mantras/affirmations
- Writing your gratitude journal
- Being more present with loved ones
- Playing with your pets
- Organising your house, things and day

MEDITATION IS YOUR GREATEST CONNECTOR

I cannot stress enough just how pivotal meditation has been to my growth. I resisted meditation for years. The sitting still, the silence, the time 'wasted'. I found the idea of it stressful and hid behind the excuse that I didn't know how to do it. But here is what I have learnt about meditation: it isn't meant to 'do' anything. Meditation simply helps you to create space and quiet. It is about connecting to your breath and being still, allowing your thoughts, problems and worries to flow past as you bathe in the stillness. Just five minutes a day can make a difference to your life.

Like all things, there are various different ways to meditate – from visualisations to walking meditations and many more. The important thing is to find what works best for you. I personally love guided meditation or meditating to music, while I have friends who say they find it helpful to repeat a mantra in their meditations, so it really is about discovering what you feel comfortable with.

Sometimes when I am meditating I get a great idea, or I gain clarity. Sometimes I sit and visualise my life as I know it can be, while some meditations are just about peace and quiet. There are times I sit there overthinking and just cannot get into it. That's OK – I just try again later or the next day. Sometimes I meditate for five minutes and sometimes twenty. That is also fine. There really is no wrong or right way.

Meditation is a powerful tool for manifesting. While you meditate, if you wish, you can visualise yourself embodying the life you dream of and sit in the feeling of what that is like. When you allow your energy to become expansive, vibrant and flowing, you become receptive to high-vibe things. (See Resources for details of my guided meditations.)

INDULGE IN LIFE'S GOOD STUFF

Nature, good literature, podcasts, music. Some of life's finer things, they can help you connect with quiet and calm, and nourish your inner core. Making more time for experiences like this will help you bring more stillness into your life. When you embrace this calm, the slower pace and the silence will reveal so much wisdom within you. The greatness of silence is unparalleled.

Seek Purpose

Start sharing your gifts now. Service is the new success.

You may have noticed (perhaps to your disappointment) that I don't spend as much time talking in this book about manifesting material possessions like watches, clothes and money as I do about your values, energy, emotions, thoughts and behaviours. That is because yes, these principles can help you attract those things, but you know what is better? Manifesting more fulfilment and joy, peace and abundance, love and purpose into your life.

Much of our desire to be approved of by others, attract cool things and strive for success comes back to our wish to be happy, right? We have this idea that possessions and the trappings of success will help us in this pursuit. But for me, we have happiness all wrong. I spent years and a hell of a lot of cash on my own hunt for fulfilment. For a long time, happiness and success looked to me like fab holidays, a cool wardrobe, a job everyone approved of, money in the bank and likes on Instagram. But nothing really ever hit the spot – I was always straight on to the next unfulfilled desire without realising that I was looking in all the wrong places. I was externalising and projecting all my happiness and purpose onto objects and people instead of understanding that it lay within.

The truth is that happiness already exists in our life, we just place limitations on our access to it. When I switched my search for happiness from things to experiences, service and a greater purpose, I realised that happiness was a by-product. A different kind of happiness, mind you – a deep, fulfilling, I-want-to-dance-around-and-tell-the-world kind. I had been searching for this deeper feeling all along. Just in the wrong places.

I truly believe I've found the formula for the kind of happiness we are all looking for. The kind that requires no input from others, no unhealthy attachments and is so profound that you don't need to move on to the next thing within minutes of receiving it because the quick fix wore off. And the formula, you ask? It is simple and has two parts:

- More service
- More purpose

THE GIFT OF GIVING

Looking back, I have always loved giving to people. Something about seeing a person's face when you do something thoughtful or show them appreciation makes me feel really good. The issue with my love of giving was that when my self-worth was on the floor, this looked like people-pleasing. It wasn't the feel-good kind of giving that I know now. My desire to make others feel happy was often to the detriment of my own happiness, as some people took advantage of it. It was fuelled by my desperation to be liked and validated by everyone else, to override the fact that I wasn't enough for me.

True service hits differently to people-pleasing. It feels different and comes from another place. Serving is when you ask how you can wholeheartedly make that person's moment/day/life better. It is saying 'yes' and offering your support when you are full of energy and have nourished yourself first. Serving is knowing that those on the receiving end will be grateful, however much or little you offer. Your desire to serve and give is not about being liked but making a difference.

Serving others is one of the most fulfilling and rewarding things you can do – and it also puts you in the perfect energy level to manifest. The more you give, the more you receive. The energy state in which serving puts us is one of the most expanded states we can be in. It is right up on the top of high-vibe living.

I learnt about the joy that it can bring in my mid-twenties. I was a personal trainer working with a wonderful woman who was originally from Australia. She came to a session one day with an envelope with 'The joy bank' written on it. Her mum in Australia had sent her some money and told her she was only allowed to spend it on something that brought her true joy. However, she had just been diagnosed with cancer and my client was about to head back to Australia to spend some time with her. She gave the envelope to me and said, 'Here, working with you has brought me so much joy, it makes sense for you to have it.' This choked me up a little and she continued, 'There is a catch, though – you're also only allowed to spend this money on something that makes you truly happy.' My initial thought was, *Perfect, I'll go buy myself some new clothes,* but then I realised how shallow that was – was that what made me really happy? I promised myself that I would spend it on something that would bring me a different kind of joy.

Many months later, I had still not spent the money. I was desperately trying to find something that would make me happy but I couldn't think of anything I could justify spending it on. Then, my client reached out to me and told me that her mum had sadly passed away, and that she was coming back to clear out her London flat before moving back to Australia to be with her family. She asked if we could do one last session as I'd been an important part of her life here.

On the morning of the session, I got her some flowers and a card to wish her well and express my condolences. As I was writing the card, I had an overwhelming sense about what to do with the money. I took the envelope she had originally given me with her mum's note and placed it inside the card – with all of the money. To see her face that day and the overwhelming love she felt when I gave her back the money, with that precious note from her mum, is something I will never forget. I learnt in that moment what giving truly is, what fulfilment really looks like and how serving someone can feel 10,000 times better than anything I had ever searched for before. I felt no loss in returning the money – nothing I could have bought myself would have topped that moment or that feeling.

Afterwards, I knew I wanted to fill up my life with more of that feeling. Today, I start each morning by asking how I can be of service to others and every time I do a workshop, host an event or start a client call, I ask how I can best serve people. There really is no greater feeling. I see it with my clients: when they talk about how they have helped someone or connected to their 'why' they light up in such a different way. When we give, we are telling the world that there is enough to go around; an unlimited amount of abundance and joy is available to all of us. Which puts us in a magical place to manifest. When we are driven by purpose and service, we completely dismantle lack, worry and fear. Our drive to help makes fear no longer an option. Giving is as high vibe as it gets, my love.

DISCOVER THE JOY OF SERVICE

These actions don't have to be grand – it could be as simple as texting a friend to tell them how important they are to you, buying someone flowers for no reason, or letting loved ones know you are there for them. Ask yourself the following questions and see how you can introduce this into your life.

- How can you bring more service into your life?
- Where can you be useful and supportive of others?

YOU HAVE A GREATER PURPOSE

Living with objects isn't the goal; living *on purpose* is. The ability to offer more service to others is largely rooted in living in your purpose. I truly believe that each and every one of us has a unique purpose here on this planet and something special to offer this world. Whether you believe it or not, you have your own unique set of gifts and talents that the world needs you to share.

Purpose is right at the top of Dr David Hawkins' scale of emotions, from low vibe to high vibe, mentioned earlier. It is one of the highest states of emotion that we can bring into our lives and therefore puts us in the perfect position to manifest our desires. The problems created by fear, sadness, discomfort, feeling stuck, lost and lacking in direction are solved by purpose. The niggles that tell us life isn't quite as it should be, the uncertainty we experience when we are lacking direction and motivation, are solved by purpose. Chasing what we want isn't the true destination of life; accessing our purpose is.

Notice how I didn't say 'finding' or 'searching' for our purpose – I said 'accessing' it. It is there, just as your gifts and talents are there; they have all simply been buried by your beliefs, your Self-sabotaging Susan and all the other crap we let get in the way of our greatness. Living without purpose, for me, is not living. Every day I feel better when I am aligned with my purpose. Every time I have a down day, a wobble or feel anxious, stressed or sad, I go back to my purpose. What I believe I was put here to do.

Your purpose is likely very closely linked to what you love to do and where your talents lie, as well as the experiences you have faced. Now, I just want to add a caveat here: your purpose doesn't have to be some sort of grand quest. You don't have to change the world. Your purpose could be anything, but it is usually linked to the service of others in some capacity – probably without you even realising it. It could be to paint beautiful paintings that bring people joy, or to help people get fitter and move better. It could be to give others a fabulous haircut or play music that makes them feel warm inside. It could be giving brands great marketing campaigns to get their message across. It doesn't have to come with huge communities, followers or clients; it could be anything – anything that makes you feel *alive and aligned*.

Trying to identify your purpose can seem overwhelming. But the key is that it feels like something you could do for hours and gives you a sense of release, and a boost like that first coffee in the morning, but better. We all have our part to play in this world and no part is smaller than another; nobody's purpose is greater than another.

No matter how often you may tell others that you aren't particularly gifted at anything, you know deep down that you have talents. We all have things that we are not so good at, things we are kinda OK at, things that we are good at and things we are pretty darn excellent at. But then we all have things we are EPIC at. That is where we want to be, ensuring that in some way we are living life as much as possible doing the things we feel we were born to do.

I really believe that my purpose in this world is to help women overcome the limitations that stop them from confidently connecting with their power and shining their light bright – and I do this through communicating. I come alive when I am creating any kind of content that serves people in this way, whether it's writing, creating podcasts or hosting talks, workshops or events. It doesn't feel like work.

Want to know the coolest thing about this? Remember when I told you how my teacher told me to stop showing off, even though my school motto was 'Let your light shine'? For years, I hid in the shadows while desperately seeking the light. The concept of shining has been a common theme throughout my life and now my purpose is rooted in helping others light up, and my business is called GETLIT. The very thing that once seemed to be my biggest obstacle has become my purpose.

FIND YOUR PURPOSE

It may take you some time and some experimentation to find your own purpose. Don't be alarmed if it doesn't come to you overnight – and don't entertain any thoughts that try to tell you that you don't have anything to offer. That's a lie and we know what to do with those lies: reframe them.

Here are some questions to help you get started:

- What are you really good at – like, super good at?
- What are you excited to learn more about?
- In what areas of life do your friends and family always come to you for support, advice or guidance?
- What can you do for hours that doesn't seem like work and makes you feel good?
- Is there anything that you feel like you were born to be doing?

Don't be afraid to be bold here. It is scary saying what you are good at, I know. But living life right at the top of the high-vibe emotion that is purpose will be your greatest magnet for all the manifesting you hope to achieve. There is no greater place.

A LITTLE WORD ON TESTS

Watch out for the tests the Universe will send you to see if you really want what you say you want.

When you begin to get clear on what you want in life and start doing the work needed to get it, the Universe will show up to test just how much you want it and how deserving you think you are of having it. I know, it's like being back at school.

The speed in which you are able to manifest your desires and create the life you want is mostly determined by whether you pass or fail the tests sent your way. Watch out for these tests, as they often show up just as you declare you are ready for something or gain clarity on what you *really* want, and the closer you get to it and the higher you raise your self-worth, the harder the tests become. They might look very similar to the desired outcome you want to manifest, yet be missing a vital ingredient. For example, you may meet someone who has a large number of the qualities you now know you want from a partner but they are missing a couple, like emotional maturity or communication, which are 'non-negotiables' for you. The Universe is asking you to prove if you really meant what you said about what you wanted.

This is your opportunity to confirm your self-worth. A chance for you to show that you really believe you are worthy of what you want – and that you trust the real deal is on its way so you're not settling for an ounce less. That is how you pass these tests. You will fail if you accept the option that is presented to you because you fear that nothing better will come along or that this will be your only chance.

When faced with tests, stand in your power and keep yourself accountable by checking in. 'Does this person/

job/item bring me fulfilment?' 'Is this manifestation as I imagined it?' If your gut tells you no, listen to it.

It can be terrifying to up-level your personal standards but the reward is far greater than the risk. When you say 'yes' only to the things you really want, you rise. Wait for the real deal and don't settle for anything less.

Final Words

Live life every single damn day knowing just how freaking powerful you are.

There you have it, my everyday principles for manifesting your best life. As you can tell by now, manifesting isn't simply a four-step 'see it, believe it, ask for it, receive it' formula. For me, everyday manifestation means living life in a way that's committed to fiercely protecting and raising your energy, without pause or question.

Problems will occur, unhappiness may still come about and challenges will undoubtedly arise when you embody this way of living – but the difference is that you, my love, will be ready. You will be armed with the tools to help you feel it all, let it go, reframe it and choose a more loving, high-vibe state of living. To connect to your immeasurable power.

The moment you put these principles in place, the Universe will work pretty quickly to make good things happen. It's almost funny at times. I have watched people gain new clarity on what they want for their business only to get a call from their ideal client the very next day. Others ask for a sign they are moving in the right direction and it's delivered within minutes. I have seen friends remove themselves from crappy situations and walk right into new ones that are for their highest good.

Get clear on what you truly want, be super specific and ask with intention. Be unapologetic about your heartfelt desires and unafraid to declare them. Always check in on the motivation behind your behaviours; watch those thoughts and be fierce about protecting that wonderful energy of yours. Then work to create more stillness, space, purpose and fulfilment in your life – and watch the fruits grow. Watch the synchronicities unfold and see the world wink at you more. Only then does the 'see it, believe it, ask for it receive it' method work.

And remember: your energy is important, so be wildly precious about devoting it to important things. Be passionate about saving it for the people, things and experiences that do nothing but make it grow and shine even brighter. Tune in to that limitless energy you once had as a child who knew that if she waved her wand and squeezed her eyes shut, her dreams would appear. Go to that light switch of yours and turn on the power. Shine in your greatness and go and get what's yours.

The principles outlined in this book have changed my life in ways I never thought possible – even while writing them down here, they have supported me – and I pray from the bottom of my heart that they do the same for you. Are you ready to let go of the version of you that doesn't believe this is possible and go write the next chapter of your story?

Because, after all, you are the author and you, my love, are powerful.

Powerful beyond measure.

Get in Touch

I truly hope that this book has inspired you and given you the tools to begin to work on your personal development, rewiring your mindset and raising your vibration.

If you feel you need some further support working through anything that has come up for you, then we have so much that will support you at GETLIT.INC. Whether you want to advance in your personal life and create a new positive mindset, find joy in your friendships and relationships or thrive in a new career and leap into entrepreneur life, our podcast, live events, online courses and masterclasses have all been designed to support you, be your hype girl and give you all the tools to get Lit and access your fullest potential.

COURSES, PROGRAMMES AND COACHING TO SUPPORT YOU FURTHER

To find out more about my four-month signature 'RISE' programme which will support you to break free from negative thinking, integrate a new belief system and embody your highest self so that you can manifest your desires, please visit: www.getlitinc.co.uk/girl-light-up

If you feel that working with a coach in a one-to-one capacity is your next step, you can apply to work with one of our accredited GETLIT coaches by visiting www.getlitinc.co.uk/work-with-a-getlit-coach

Or you can also visit our directory of coaches at www.getlitinc.co.uk/expert-directory

FURTHER RESOURCES TO HELP YOU WITH YOUR MANIFESTATIONS AND DEVELOPMENT

To access a ten-minute meditation to help you visualise your manifestations as well as a quiz to see how close to your manifestations you are, please visit www.getlitinc.co.uk/you-are-powerful

To see our full list of courses, programmes, workshops and resources to help you excel in your business, career or personal development, head to www.getlitinc.co.uk.

The 'Get Lit with Becki' podcast is available on Apple podcasts, Acast, Spotify and SoundCloud.

To keep up to date with what I am doing or to find out about one-to-one mentoring, head to www.beckirabin.com and be sure to get social by following me on Instagram: @beckirabin and Get Lit @getlitinc

Further Reading

Books have always been and will continue to be an essential tool for my growth. Below are some of the titles that I mention in this book as well as some that have been fundamental in shaping my journey.

I hope they do the same for you.

Dr Wayne W. Dyer, *There 'Is a Spiritual Solution to Every Problem* (Thorsons, 2002)

Dr Joe Dispenza, *Becoming Supernatural: How Common People Are Doing the Uncommon* (Hay House, 2017)

Louise L. Hay, *You Can Heal Your Life* (Hay House, 1984)

Esther and Jerry Hicks, *Ask and It is Given: Learning to Manifest Your Desires* (Hay House, 2005)

Jen Senciro, *You are a Badass: How To Stop Doubting Your Greatness and Start Living an Awesome Life* (John Murray, 2016)

Alan Cohen, *A Course in Miracles Made Easy: Mastering the Journey from Fear to Love* (Hay House, 2015)

Gabrielle Bernstein, *The Universe Has Your Back: Transform Fear to Faith* (Hay House, 2016)

Gaye Hendricks, *The Big Leap: Conquer Your Hidden Fear and Take Life to the Next Level* (HarperOne, 2010)

Melissa Ambrosini, *Mastering Your Mean Girl: The No-BS Guide to Silencing Your Inner Critic and Becoming Wildly Wealthy, Fabulously Healthy and Bursting with Love* (Tarcher, 2016)

Vex King, *Good Vibes, Good Life: How Self-Love Is The Key To Unlocking Your Greatness* (Hay House, 2018)

Gabrielle Bernstein, *Super Attractor: Methods for Manifesting a Life Beyond Your Wildest Dreams* (Hay House, 2019)

Dr David R. Hawkins, *Power Vs Force: The Hidden Determinants of Human Behaviour* (Hay House, 2014)

Eckhart Tolle, *The Power Of Now: A Guide to Spiritual Enlightenment* (Namaste Publishing, 1997)

Rhonda Byrne, *The Secret* (Simon & Schuster, 2006)

Acknowledgements

To my two rocks: Mamma and Sista – I quite possibly do not know where I would be without you both always cheering me on. Thank you, from the bottom of my heart, for showing me strength and teaching me courage I never knew was possible, reminding me every single day how capable and deserving I am of shining.

Dad, I truly hope I have made you proud and I thank you for being by my side while I was writing these pages; I felt your guidance and light the whole time.

To my GETLIT community – clients, and colleagues – I cannot thank you enough for trusting me with your growth and helping me on my mission to spread the message to women that it *is* safe to light up. I am truly the luckiest girl in the world to have such a vibrant, supportive and badass community.

To my best pals (you know who you are), who have been by my side through thick and thin – through the tears, through the challenges that I faced personally – I am forever blessed to have such incredible people in my life.

A special thank you to my little Georgie. I will always remember having you by my side every day while writing this book, reminding me in the moments of doubts that I had what it takes and I could do it.

Writing this book during a worldwide pandemic was a blessing that I am so very grateful for. In this incredibly difficult time for us all, it quite literally gave me purpose, reminded me to have hope and helped me stay lit.

Thank you to my agent Valeria for supporting my vision from the beginning and Sam and Laura and the team at Ebury for believing in me and giving me the opportunity to share my words with the world and begin my dream journey as an author.

I would also like to personally acknowledge and thank the Universe for sending every single hardship, challenge and lesson I have faced my way. Every single tear gave me a deeper desire to do my work.

This book is dedicated to all of you incredible women that I see every day putting in the work to rise up to your higher self. You truly inspire me more than you know. In the moments that I ever doubt or question myself and go to sit down, you guys get me back up from the shadows and help me shine my own light.

All my love and light,

B x

Index

Notes

BECKI RABIN

Becki Rabin is a business mentor, empowerment coach and serial entrepreneur with a passion for self-development and an obsession with helping others unlock their fullest potential. On a mission to help women raise their vibration, own their power and create a mindset that will take them places so that they can manifest their dream life, Becki has over a decade's experience in the wellness industry. She is the host of the 'Get Lit with Becki' podcast and the founder of GETLIT™, the community dedicated to your business, personal and professional development.

MORE NOW AGE ESSENTIALS